SEEING VIETNAM

ENCOUNTERS OF THE ROAD AND HEART

SUSAN BROWNMILLER

HarperCollins*Publishers*

HarperCollins books may be purchased for educational, business, or sales promotional use. For information please write: Special Markets Department, HarperCollins Publishers, Inc., 10 East 53rd Street, New York, NY 10022.

FIRST EDITION

Designed by C. Linda Dingler
Map by Paul Pugliese

Library of Congress Cataloging-in-Publication Data
Brownmiller, Susan.
  Seeing Vietnam : encounters of the road and heart / Susan Brownmiller.—1st ed.
    p.   cm.
  ISBN 0-06-019049-3
  1. Vietnam—Description and travel. 2. Brownmiller, Susan—Journeys—Vietnam. I. Title.
DS556.39.B74 1994
915.9704'44—dc20   93-47691

94 95 96 97 98 ❖/HC 10 9 8 7 6 5 4 3 2 1

CONTENTS

PREFACE

In November 1992 I went to Vietnam on a magazine assignment to explore the country from a tourist's point of view. Scenery, hotel accommodations, restaurants, a cruise down a picturesque river to a quaint pagoda—my purview would be what a first-time traveler usually sees of a distant, unknown country, and I was surely a first-time traveler. On our side, travel restrictions had recently been lifted for ordinary Americans. On their side, they were getting more relaxed about pesky, inquisitive foreigners who wanted to go hither and yon, where they might spend a few dollars. They were opening up to a market economy, readying for a brave new future. Signs were in the air that our trade embargo soon would be lifted as well.

So it was a grandly adventurous time to be entering Vietnam on an American passport, to have a purposeful mission that carried a minimum of emotional freight, to look through fresh, open eyes at the skinny, curving strip of Southeast Asia that had haunted us since the mid-sixties.

The truth was, I'd checked out of Vietnam emotionally a long time ago. I had ceased to follow its fortunes sometime after the 1968 Tet Offensive, had renewed my interest during the 1973 Paris peace talks, then dropped it again until those awesome shots on TV of the last helicopters leaving Saigon. We need our defense mechanisms, and mine had been to disengage from the horror by skipping the news stories, by turning the page.

From 1965 to 1968 I hadn't had a choice. I was a network newswriter for the American Broadcasting Company, a minor cog in the apparatus that brought the televised war into our nation's living rooms. In those years I handled a Vietnam story every day—screening film, editing sequences, writing intros in New York for our correspondents based in Saigon. My job was to carve one minute and thirty seconds for an 11:00 p.m. feed to our affiliated stations from outtakes that didn't make the prime-time news. I slogged through routine search-and-destroy operations and inconclusive firefights, pieced together murky footage of falling black bombs, raging smoke and fire, whirring med-evac Hueys, wounded GIs on stretchers, captured enemy in black pajamas, burning monks, screaming children fleeing across fields, women keening their dead. I cut airable snippets from hollow assurances by Lyndon Johnson and General William Westmoreland about the light at the end of the tunnel.

I disliked my job and I hated the war. So I quit in the strange, strange year of '68, an epochal time when a vast, ugly boil burst on the American body politic, when Martin Luther King and Robert Kennedy were felled by assassins, when peace marches turned violent and rioting students closed down Columbia, when rock, dope, and sex became urgent soporifics, when President Johnson, a focus of hate, chose not to run again and the Democratic Convention tore apart in Chicago.

Vietnam receded from my frontal lobes, but it did not go away. The final death tally on the memorial wall in Washington inscribed the names of more than fifty-eight thousand Americans. In the land of the conflagration perhaps two million had died. And when it was over, it wasn't over. There was Pol Pot in Cambodia, an invasion by the Vietnamese army, and border skirmishes with China. To keep the recurring nightmare out of my head, I found reasons to be angry with the Vietnamese. I got cross with them for remaining so warlike when I thought they should have stayed pitiful. Later on, I bore them a grudge for the Boat People.

Twenty years ago, Vietnam was the battleground of sharp ideological conflicts in the international arena. Those conflicts have lost most of their currency in the new world order, but the reunified nation remains frozen in time in the American perception, its power to reactivate old traumas and suspicions unfaded despite the realities of the post–Cold War era. Ready to take the plunge, I wanted to see the country in peacetime, its problems and progress, but I knew I'd be stepping into a mirror to face the jutting fractures of two countries linked by a tragic past. As I gathered research matter and advice from friends of friends who'd actually been there, I began plotting my route.

Photographer Maggie Steber was shooting a story in Oklahoma when we spoke by phone and introduced ourselves, arranging a link-up on the cab ride out to JFK airport, the earliest we could meet. She sounded game and adventurous, a thorough professional. Traveling light was the way to go, we agreed, with good walking shoes, antimalaria tablets, rain gear, sun screen, and something warm, a sleeveless down vest or a sweater, for Hanoi. She fretted about the extra weight of her cameras, lenses, tripod, plus a couple of hundred rolls of film and an all-purpose medicine kit. I would be toting a notebook.

Under Vietnam's arcane rules, we required a "sponsor" to secure our travel permits. Our status as journalists looking into tourism put us in a peculiar limbo. We needed to cover a lot of ground efficiently, but we shared a strong aversion to the packaged, conducted tour. The notion of special favors and close scrutiny from a government press attaché or a flunky in the ministry of tourism was equally repugnant, but we didn't want to get expelled from the country for fibbing about our intentions, either.

There was, it turned out, an intermediate solution. Foreign investors were flocking to Vietnam to explore the possibilities of its offshore oil fields. In its wisdom, the government had set up an agency to cosset the business people with translators and sightseeing junkets. The tail had begun to wag the dog, and the oil-services agency was accepting clients whose reasons for poking about fell short of a stake in Vietnam crude. Through InnerAsia Expeditions, an American travel company in San Francisco, we applied for regular tourist visas and submitted our proposed itinerary to the oil-services outfit. It came back approved: a private, customized tour for two from Hanoi to the Mekong Delta.

We were embarking on the trip of a lifetime, a journey that would take us full circle, forward to once forbidden places and back into memory. "And hey," Maggie joked, "we might even knock off a few pounds."

HANOI

There's always an extra alertness on the road coming in from the airport. I sit rigid in my seat, leaning forward. Yes, there are green patches of rice fields, some dumpy concrete-block shacks. What I fix on, however, are the amateurishly lettered signs in a roman alphabet that is standard written Vietnamese.

COM PHO. Rice, Soup. Welcoming indications of roadside restaurants in those concrete-block shacks.

One sign stands out because we pass it so often. It must be important. This will be my first clue to the cultural state of the nation, or at least of Hanoi.

XE MAY.

"What's that, Mr. Kha?" I ask urgently. "What does that sign say?" I pronounce it "she-may," pleased that I know a thing or two about Chinese phonetics, and figuring that pinyin will help me read Vietnamese aloud.

"Say-mai," he says, correcting me.

"What does it mean?"

"Motorcycle," he says dismissively. "They repair."

And so the first entry I make in my Vietnam notebook, written in a shaky hand as we cruise along the highway, is "XE MAY = MOTORCYCLE REPAIR."

There is a natural progression in the late-twentieth-century development of Southeast Asian cities that is akin to the rebirth of a forest. First there are bicycles, next come the motor scooters. The third stage of development—ah, the longed-for apex of civilization, material wealth, and modern industrial progress—is the private car. Judging from the number of XE MAY signs, Hanoi is approaching Stage 2, the motor scooters, which break down often.

Our spotless new white Nissan has little competition on the highway, except for the occasional truck. The traffic is so light that we yell "Stop!" so Maggie can get out and photograph a Buddhist funeral procession with huge banners that is wending its way on the road's shoulder. Their ceremonies over, the mourners are returning to their village to enjoy the baskets of food they have ritually offered to the departed. They're in a jovial mood as the Western woman goes into her paparazzi routine.

I've read somewhere about the docility of the Northerners, supposedly pushed around so much that they'll put up with anything, but I don't think that's what's going on here. I think the mourners are enjoying the unexpected oddity of Maggie. She's an event for them as much as they're an event for us. Foreigners have funny customs.

Le Duc Kha is the full name of our guide, but we are to call him Mr. Kha. I don't know why he prefers the distancing honorific "Mister," unless for reasons of pride, since he calls us Maggie and Susan. He's a few years younger than I am, but in the ten days we spend together, he remains Mr. Kha, and takes on a "Mr. Kha" personality when I begin to write about him. Mr. Kha wears glasses, which is rare for a Vietnamese. Not that their eyesight is better than ours, as a nation, but because eyeglasses cost three weeks' wages for the average worker.

Mr. Kha bears up under us beautifully. Well, we have to

put up with him, too. And each other. As he gets to know us better, he insists on telling dumb sex jokes that make him giggle, like the one about the Japanese man and the beautiful prostitute who take off their clothes. . . . "Banzai!" he shouts, advancing. "Bonsai," she replies, pointing. I'll say this for Mr. Kha, I didn't always get the punch lines, but I can still recall his infectious, high-pitched laughter. The laughter served a useful diplomatic purpose. We were unusually insistent, assertive American women.

"The program starts tomorrow morning," Mr. Kha announced in the Metropole's lobby, after watching us change money and seeing that we were properly checked in.

I had pulled one string, and one string only, for Vietnam, and that was to get myself into the Metropole. Hanoi's legendary hostelry, the creation of the same Blouet family that ran the George V in Paris, had opened its doors in 1911 at a proud, expansive moment in French colonial rule. Vietnam was paying for itself very nicely, from coal mines in the north to the Michelin rubber plantations in the south, and tucked everywhere else, rice fields for profitable exports. Within two years the Continental opened for business in Saigon, offering a second oasis for elite colonials and sophisticated travelers shuttling between the two cities. Somerset Maugham had relaxed at both hotels during his Indochina travels, and so had Graham Greene.

The Metropole had fallen on hard times after the French abruptly departed in 1954, in the wake of their stunning defeat at Dien Bien Phu. Operated as the state-owned Thong Nhat (the name pointedly meant "Reunification"), the hotel soon boasted a resident population of rats that outnumbered the tourists. A few years ago Pullman-Sofitel, the French hotel conglomerate, made a judicious settlement with the Blouet heirs. On March 31, 1992, the famous landmark was triumphantly reopened under a 48-52 percent joint venture with Hanoi's tourist authority, the four points favoring the Vietnamese. Working from old pictures, Pullman had lovingly restored the green-shuttered, white colonial facade, put down new Vietnamese marble in the lobby, and totally refurbished the gutted interior except for the fine atrium stairwell and the hardwood floors. The infamous rats were gone, and with them, according to some misty-eyed traditionalists, a lot of the charm (they particularly missed the old-fashioned ceiling fans). Already there was a three-month waiting list for coveted reservations at the chic ninety-room wonder that proclaimed, "Ooo-la-la, the French are back!"

Not stay at the Metropole? Why, that would be like skipping the Peninsula in Hong Kong, the Oriental in Bangkok, Raffles in Singapore, pearls of the Orient that I knew only from sitting in their lobbies. What kind of sophisticated international traveler was I? Gritting my teeth, I had called Pullman's public relations woman in New York, explained the high purpose of my visit, and begged for two single rooms ($150 a night plus 10 percent government tax), which the magazine would pay for. "You *want* me to stay at the Metropole," I wheedled. They agreed, and when two cancellations came up, we were in.

When Maggie and I were shown to our quarters, she got a front room with a view and a balcony, and I got a back room facing some demolition and construction. "That's right, because I've got to photograph that darling little park across the way," the ingrate said sweetly.

We oohed and aahed over the polished granite counter surface in our bathrooms, the porcelain sink bearing the trademark Jacob Delafon (the same company that had manufactured the originals), the hair dryer, the money safe, the temperature controls, the mini-bar and fridge stocked with beer, imported nibbles, and free mineral water, the basket of fruit and the flowers, the digital phone, the fax capability, the cable TV that gave us a choice of local programming, the BBC World Service, rock videos from MTV, or a movie.

Giggling, we tried on the red satin lounging robes embroidered "Pullman Metropole." Suddenly feeling the tug of traditionalism ourselves, we wished that they hadn't added "Pullman," which they'd emblazoned as well on the hotel's front canopy and on their fleet of three-wheeled cyclos lined up at the entrance. But why cavil? Pullman had something to crow about. Unlike the Trump Plaza.

I deposited my large-denomination U.S. bills and a huge stack of dong in the safe. The South Vietnamese piastre had inflated wildly during the war; the dong was far less volatile today. At ten thousand to the dollar (an average day's wages in Vietnam), I was loaded with local currency although I'd changed only fifty bucks. Because of our trade embargo, I couldn't use an American credit card in Vietnam, but American dollars were the prime medium of exchange.

Everything at the Metropole was priced in dollars. A cup of coffee was $2.50. I could order a bottle of Dom Perignon from Room Service for $179, or Veuve Cliquot for a comparable price, if I desired. A modest bottle of Chardonnay was $29.75. Resting in a wicker tray on the mini-bar, a small bag of peanuts gaily packaged in Singapore was $3.25. A mini-bag of potato chips was $3.50. Compared to the real world outside the hotel—which I was about to discover—these prices were astounding.

It was late afternoon. I slipped some singles and a wad of dong into my wallet and set off to explore the winding streets of the Old Quarter.

Broadly speaking, two categories of Americans had spent time in Hanoi during the war. The first group consisted of POWs, including airmen flying reconnaissance missions and bombing sorties over the city who'd been downed by Soviet-made antiaircraft guns and surface-to-air missiles. Pilots who survived a direct hit had sat out the rest of the war, along with POWs captured in more distant locales, in converted city prisons. The largest and most notorious of the jails, the Hoa Lo (meaning "oven"), had acquired the sardonic nickname "Hanoi Hilton."

To the Vietnamese, the most famous POW in the Hanoi Hilton was navy lieutenant commander John McCain, son of the commander of American naval forces in the Pacific, whose Douglas A-4 Skyhawk was shot down on October 26, 1967. McCain ejected from the aircraft, breaking both arms and a leg in the wind shear, and bailed out into West Lake at the northern end of the city. He was dragged from the water by the local militia, who proceeded to shout and kick at his crumpled body, as he recalled, until regular soldiers arrived to take him away.

The mind-boggling symbolism of his plunge—an event comparable to a Luftwaffe pilot dropping into the Central Park reservoir during a 1943 blitzkrieg, to be fished out by angry patriots of Central Park West—was not lost on the citizens of Hanoi, who erected a monument on the shores of West Lake marking the site of his capture.

Later, when I stood at the stone sculpture of a broken wing and a parachuting airman, which identifies McCain incorrectly as an air force major, I thought of the lines

> *Icarus and his father Daedalus flew from Crete*
> *on wings of wax.*
> *He flew too near the sun.*

The wax melted,
He fell into the sea.

McCain was flying his twenty-third mission from the U.S.S. *Oriskany* in the South China Sea. He was diving in on a hydroelectric power station when his wing was clipped by a surface-to-air missile.

Released from captivity at the end of the war, McCain settled in Arizona and was elected to Congress as a conservative Republican. The third-generation navy man applied his hard-won expertise to POW-MIA affairs, returning to Hanoi on investigative missions requiring the cooperation of the Vietnamese government.

Former POW John McCain is now United States Senator John McCain. In January 1993 he sided with a Senate panel report finding no compelling evidence that missing servicemen were still alive in Indochina. It was the right thing to do—the *factually* right thing to do, and a crucial step on the road that would lead eventually to full normalization of relations with the Vietnamese—but emotions on the MIA issue run high. McCain says that some MIA families accuse him "of being everything from a traitor to the Manchurian Candidate, and that isn't likely to change."

The celebrity quotient of the second category of Americans to land in Hanoi during the war had been part and parcel of their quixotic mission. These were the assorted doves who flew in, via Paris and Phnom Penh, as invited guests of the Hanoi government. From Mary McCarthy and Susan Sontag, intellectuals of impeccable standing, to Jane Fonda, Tom Hayden, Joan Baez, and former attorney general Ramsey Clark, they'd sought the limelight of controversy in frustration and moral outrage. Convinced that America was wrong to be fighting in Southeast Asia, they gave voice to their fury through a fine-tuned sense of political drama.

Mary McCarthy visited North Vietnam's capital in 1968, and tried to put together a group of the prominent and the famous who would in effect be willing hostages to American bombs. Joan Baez returned home with a POW. Carried away by her Joan of Arc persona, Fonda beamed radio broadcasts to GIs, interviewed prisoners in the Hanoi Hilton, and posed for photographs on top of an antiaircraft gun. Depending on their prior attitudes and/or their evolving emotions, Americans were startled, impressed, put off, or angered by the nervy grandstanding of the celebrity doves. Fonda was hounded for years by unforgiving right-wing fringe groups screaming "Hanoi Jane."

But hey, I'm a legal tourist in 1992, and my trepidation in stepping out of my hotel rests exclusively on my atrocious sense of direction. On the map the Old Quarter was a mere few blocks from the Metropole. For me that meant heading up the street due north and stopping in panic at the first intersection. Holding my ground at the corner, I importuned passers-by with "Old City? Old City?"

A few years ago, the sight of a Westerner in Hanoi brought cries of "*Lien Xo*" ("Russian") from small children, or sometimes—my, did she make an impression—"Jane Fonda!" No longer. Concerned pedestrians gathered to examine my map. A cyclo driver beckoned, hoping for a fare. A smartly dressed woman drew up on her bicycle to help with her limited English. With everyone's goodwill, I was sent on my way.

What's the attitude toward Americans in Hanoi? Friendly. Very friendly.

Nothing makes me happier than an outdoor market where I can snorkel quietly, pretending to be invisible, lured further and further by strange, wondrous foodstuffs and bright-colored wares. Hanoi's Old Quarter, a maze of streets lined by

dilapidated houses with sagging terraces, was spilling over
with fruit, fish, vegetables, flowers, shoes, paper gifts for the
dead, cheap wind-up toys, and golden-haired plastic dolls in
party dresses. At the end of a cul-de-sac a woman was selling
blue-and-white bowls and jars from a stall. A repertoire of
dragon, lotus, bamboo, and chrysanthemum designs announced
that her ceramics were from the kilns of Bat Trang.

Bat Trang village, only a short drive from Hanoi, was on
my list of places to visit, but I didn't want to wait to negotiate my first economic transaction in Vietnam and try out my
skills in a bargaining culture. I selected a medium-sized
incense pot brush-painted with fighting dragons. Glazed pots
of this size and larger are filled with sand to hold burning joss
sticks on Buddhist altars. Mine, I figured, could have a useful
secular life as a pencil holder, or perhaps as a cachepot for a
plant back home.

My experience of foreign travel is that you'll never go
hungry or fail to make a purchase if people have something
they want to sell. Language barriers fall away in restaurants
and shops. Pantomime is an international art form. Communication is at its most intense. The Bat Trang merchant
indicated four thousand dong. Pretending alarm, I shook my
head and held up two fingers. She countered with three.
Sold! She carefully wrapped the pot in old paper, happy for
the sale.

Later on, I was struck with remorse. I had paid thirty cents
American, knocking ten cents off the asking price. There was
a vague moral line between playing the dumb tourist who
gets rooked in a bargaining culture and depriving a street
seller of one dime in an economically squeezed, impoverished
country, particularly when I might be tempted to gobble a
$3.25 bag of peanuts at the Metropole. Oh, did those peanuts
on the mini-bar torment me! They represented free enter-

prise in the heart of Hanoi, while our government was still lobbying to keep Vietnam out of the World Bank and the International Monetary Fund, out of the aid loop for development loans.

Although I continued to bargain whenever I could, mostly with street hawkers and cyclo drivers, I never shook the feeling that the good-natured interplay was mildly inappropriate for a middle-class American relatively flush with dollars. Furthermore, my bargaining worked only with the poorer strata of the population unfamiliar with free-spending Westerners and international exchange rates. Cannier merchants pitching their goods to tourists hewed resolutely to a two-tiered system.

I couldn't knock anything off my next transaction, so I stood by the stall and watched the brisk business in socks and underpants until I determined that the fair local price for two pairs of cotton briefs, one blue, one olive drab, truly was eighty cents. Another excellent purchase teeming with social significance. The stitched-in labels read "USA," and in smaller letters, "Made in V.N."

If I'd had a spray can and a spare empty wall, here's the graffito I would have scrawled: "France loves Vietnam, but Vietnam loves the USA." I suppose it's the nature of love, at least among nations, to go unrequited.

For dinner we'd booked reservations at 202 Hue, a privately owned restaurant known by its street address, which we'd heard was a favorite hangout for the diplomatic community. I conjured an image of dark wood paneling, white damask napkins, table hopping, whispered intrigues. The photographer was taking no chances; she was a vision in leather camera bags and pastel chiffon. Stepping past the fleet of cyclos emblazoned "Pullman," we struck a price with a couple of drivers around the corner.

Cyclos are three-wheeled open carriages powered by the

driver's leg muscles. Small Vietnamese women and children can pile in two or three to a carriage, but one American seemed like a fair enough load. After bumping along a boulevard in a southerly direction for approximately fifteen minutes, we drew up to the curb in front of a luncheonette.

Sensing our confusion, the drivers emphatically waved us inside. A knowing waiter directed us up a flight of stairs, where the decor in the crowded front and back rooms was still luncheonette. Waiters bearing bottles of beer and trays of cracked crab bustled among the Formica tables, where the happy diners, dressed like workingmen, not diplomats, hailed them with appreciative noises. We were shown to a table and handed a mimeographed menu in plastic. From a column in English we selected fresh crab fried with garlic and salt.

I expect to have a credibility problem here, because I'm going to say that the garlic-fried crab was the best crab I've ever eaten, and that includes cracked crab in Maryland and crab cakes at the Coach House in Greenwich Village. I continued to eat crab nearly every day I was in Vietnam, and quickly learned the word for it (*cua*, pronounced "cooa"), but even when I veered in other directions, say to fried prawns, what I put in my mouth was extraordinarily delicious.

We gorged on the crabs and eyed the bananas flambé at another table, suffused with those ineffable feelings of warmth and belonging that are aroused by a good meal and a full stomach. Once, years ago in Paris, when I topped off a dinner at La Coupole with a huge dessert, a Frenchman at the next table loudly announced to his companion, "The appetite of tourists is *formidable!*"

When the bill came, it was 130,000 dong, enormous until we remembered that it came to $13, including beer and a can of imported Coca-Cola. Maggie counted out thirteen ten-thousand-dong notes, which relieved her wallet of some of its bulk. The waiter rapidly recounted, deftly folding the tenth note over the preceding nine, a ritual that would become familiar to us. A ten-thousand-dong note was the largest denomination I saw in Vietnam. Eventually I decided that it might be easier for everyone at the high-priced tourist spots if we paid in dollars. Four months later the state bank began issuing larger denominations.

While we were eating we were joined by Barbara Cohen— Dr. Barbara Cohen, a renowned member of Hanoi's tiny American expatriate community, although her status, she informed me in a rush of words, was rather tenuous at the moment. Barbara and her husband had graduated from med school in the late sixties and signed up for a tour of duty with the U.S. Army Medical Corps. From 1970 to 1971 she had served as a psychiatrist with the Ninety-fifth Evacuation Hospital in Danang, better known today as China Beach.

Vietnam had been her transforming experience. She had returned several times after the peace accords to research and write, in 1990, the first postwar guidebook by an American. Unable to wrench herself away, she had started a novel set in Vietnam, immersing herself in Buddhist customs, making intense friendships among artists and young people intrigued by her presence.

Barbara's marriage had recently broken up over her Vietnam obsession. And now the Hanoi government was getting sticky about extending her visa, as confused as her husband about why a doctor would throw up her formal training to live far from home in a decrepit hotel room with a word processor, wear *ao dai*s (long-sleeved tunics and flowing trousers), eat on the cheap, and poke her nose inquisitively wherever she could, practically to "go native."

I found her to be a tiny whirlwind of enthusiasms, delightfully appealing, a gold mine of cultural information, and not at all paranoid, as I had begun to fear, once she calmed down and explained her visa problems. The woman was nuts about Vietnam and wished to be a writer, not a doctor—a personal aspiration not uncommon among individualistic Americans. The paranoia was entirely Vietnam's.

Her wavy grey-blond hair, volubility, and diminutive stature reminded me of someone I knew. She was a ringer for Barbara Garson, a neighbor of mine in Greenwich Village, who had written *MacBird* in 1965 while a graduate student at Berkeley. *MacBird* opened in New York in 1967, with Stacy Keach in a starring role, and became the first antiwar play of the Vietnam generation. By 1969 Barbara Garson was a full-time movement activist, working at a "GI coffeehouse" near Tacoma, Washington, where the idea was to provide a friendly countercultural setting for enlisted men at Fort Lewis who'd come in and rap about their feelings toward the war. She handed out conscientious-objector applications to draftees, found lawyers for draft resisters, and generally tried to make rebels out of working-class youth who had been inducted. At the height of the GI coffee-house movement, antiwar activists were running twelve establishments near stateside military bases.

Dr. Barbara Cohen, on the other hand, had volunteered for her stint in Vietnam with no special feelings about the war, only the notion that a job in an exotic corner of the world would be a chance-of-a-lifetime romantic adventure.

With a flourish she hands me her business card, which reads "Cultural Writer and Researcher, Tourism Consultant," and introduces her eighteen-year-old assistant, Le Phuong Anh, a business student who is acquiring some on-the-job training. Phuong Anh's card, offered with her own proud flourish, says "English-Vietnamese Interpreter, Tourism and Business Guide."

And then, with great merriment, we pile into some cyclos to taste the social life of young Hanoi on a Saturday night.

The building is monstrously large and modern, a white concrete edifice with a huge front ramp and a colonnade resembling hydroelectric-station smokestacks somewhere in the Urals. On my map it's identified as the Vietnam–Soviet Union Friendship Cultural Palace. I should have guessed. We duck into a side entrance and dart down a long, empty hall to find a makeshift refreshment stand serving soft drinks, a card table with a money box and a roll of tickets, and three teenagers collecting an admittance fee.

Inside a bare rectangular room lined with folding chairs, twenty young couples are twirling around a dance floor . . . doing the tango. No strobe lights and only the most rudimentary of sound systems, a reel-to-reel squawk box, but I am definitely in a Hanoi disco. Cued by the taped music, the dancers change partners, segueing effortlessly into a polka, a waltz, the lambada. I focus on one sympatico team, a Fred Astaire and Ginger Rogers who nimbly range over the dance floor, strutting and dipping through intricate turns. I am struck by their studious aplomb, their utter seriousness of purpose. Maybe not Fred and Ginger. Closer to Vernon and Irene Castle, for there is something quaintly dated about these ever so modern youth of Hanoi in their short, flaring dresses and freshly pressed shirts, even when they break unexpectedly into the twist.

"What's going on?" I ask Barbara Cohen when she returns out of breath from a spirited polka.

"Very authentic. No Westerners come here. The kids took over the Friendship Club after the Russians left. They learned the steps from a Czech diplomat who taught ballroom dancing in Prague."

"Oh," I say. "*Oh!*"

Soon I am on my feet, joining a circle that is twisting chastely in the dim light. Shyly I fling out an arm. My shoulder-strap bag swings to a rhythm of its own. Well, I think, I am neither the first nor the last conspicuous American in Vietnam.

The music breaks off at 10:00 p.m. Hanoi is an early-to-bed, early-to-rise kind of town.

Back at the hotel, faint tinkling sounds of laughter from a private party in the garden waft up to my room. A male voice is crooning, "*Bes-ameeeee, besame mucho*" as I drift off to sleep.

One reality of Vietnam that must be factored into all equations is its tremendous population explosion. Everyone in the disco, for example, was too young to remember the American war.

I have a chart from the latest available population census, indicating that nearly two-thirds of the country's seventy-two million inhabitants are under thirty. Political power, on the other hand, is held mainly by old men who have their dreams and their memories. As America recently chose a president in his forties—a man young enough, wise enough, to have made a personal decision not to fight in the war—Vietnam, eventually, will be led by a generation with no firsthand experience in throwing off the conqueror's yoke, the primary occupation during the lifetime of its current leaders.

Physically, Hanoi charms a visitor with tree-lined boulevards and gemlike lakes set in leafy green parks. There are enough stucco row houses and ochre villas with blue louver shutters and iron filigree gates to have given Somerset Maugham the impression, in the 1920s, that he was in a

French provincial town, perhaps Grenoble or Montpelier.

Known at its inception as Thang Long, or Rising Dragon, Hanoi became Vietnam's imperial capital in the year 1010, at the start of the Ly dynasty. By legend, a Ly prince selected the site after watching a golden dragon rise up from a bend in the mighty Red River. The original citadel was laid out according to the ancient Chinese rules of geomancy, or harmonic balance with nature, in three concentric enclosures—a common people's city, a mandarin city, and at the center a Forbidden City containing the royal palace. Beyond the citadel, a complex system of dikes and canals sprang up to control the annual floodwaters and regulate the rice plains of the Red River Delta. There are those who say that of all the factors that conspired to make the Vietnamese so enduring, the most important was the continual struggle against the floodwaters to provide a sufficiency of grain, because it instructed a hardy, determined people in the sensitive art of working together.

After the French occupation in 1883, most of Hanoi's original architecture was razed and replaced by European buildings in a neo-provincial or neo-Parisian mode. French architects also incorporated Vietnamese or Chinese roof elements in an eclectic East-West amalgam that came to be known as "Norman pagoda." Today it's often hard to determine the provenance of a particular building, but in the seventy years since Maugham made his off-the-cuff observation, Hanoi's reminders of the colonial presence have acquired a rare, faded beauty. On a sunny day, streets in the older parts of town are a pastel gouache of pink, blue, lemon, and sand.

Beset by other problems, Hanoi's city government has not made urban renewal a high priority. Exquisite but crumbling facades badly in need of renovation teem with vibrant life—storefront shops, children at play, a pot of bougainvillaea on a sagging balcony. The urge is to cry out, "There's where I'll rent my garret!" until one remembers that there is no central heating during Hanoi's cold winters, that the night-soil collector makes his rounds in lieu of indoor plumbing. The best of the villas, grandiose wonders erected on spacious grounds to house the colonial administration, serve today as government buildings and museums.

A piece of the historic patrimony from the Ly dynasty, Van Mieu, or the Temple of Literature, is still standing. Strolling with Mr. Kha through the eleventh-century ruins—a gate, a pond, a temple, and the walls of several pavilions—I began to understand something of Hanoi's sense of entitlement and pride.

Van Mieu, a mandarin university based on the Chinese Confucian model, was erected in 1070 during the reign of Emperor Ly Thang Tong. Scholars lived in its wooden dorms, walked its paved courtyards, studied in its famous library, and declaimed their original verse from the Poet's Balcony before they underwent six weeks of grueling baccalaureate examinations. Van Mieu's graduates, the crème de la crème of the emperor's civil service, had their names inscribed in Chinese characters on stone tablets in the courtyard. Eighty-two of the steles, each resting on a stone tortoise, stand like gravestones today. After their intensive training, the mandarin scholars were dispersed to the far reaches of the kingdom, where they took up administrative posts. Lower-level mandarins, who did not come to the capital for advanced study, filled more modest rungs in the civil service, such as village magistrate and teacher. Early in the nineteenth century, after the southern Nguyens defeated the northern Trinhs, Emperor Gia Long closed Van Mieu and replaced it with a new national mandarin university in his newly created imperial capital of Hue. During the colonial period the French administrative bureaucracy took over the vacant Van Mieu complex and jokingly called it the Palace of Crows for the flocks of birds that nested in the rafters. Van Mieu was the site of several pitched battles between the French and the Viet Minh in the independence wars of the 1940s and 1950s, when much of it was destroyed by French bombs.

Mr. Kha was perplexed time and again by what was meaningful to an American tourist, what resonated for me with historic significance, what passed me by in my forgetfulness or ignorance. Crossing the Red River the first day coming in from the airport, he had pointed to a steel-girdered bridge, a patchy span seemingly constructed in many styles, running parallel to the new bridge that we were taking.

"Long Bien. You knew it as Doumer Bridge," he offered.

Did I? I racked my brain. "Uh, named for the French governor?" I floundered.

Hah! The kind of guess that might squeak by on *Jeopardy.* Paul Doumer had been the French architect of Vietnam's colonization, the governor-general who said, "When France arrived in Indochina, the Annamites were ripe for servitude." When Doumer arrived in 1897, he proceeded to put servitude to work for the mother country by encouraging the massive conscription of landless peasants who labored as near-slaves for colonial mines and plantations.

French engineers completed the construction of Paul Doumer Bridge in 1902. A remarkable feat for its day, the mile-long span with pilings one hundred feet deep tamed the Red River with an auto lane and a railroad track. It was the grandest bridge in Asia. To the Vietnamese, Doumer Bridge was a humbling symbol and an all too real example of the conqueror's powers. Those who held to the old superstitions had predicted that the terrible, feared dragon who lived in the river would never permit such a violation of his territorial space. (Dragons are a bit overworked in Vietnamese mythology, but so be it.) The symbolism of Doumer Bridge was diametrically reversed in 1954 when Viet Minh soldiers proudly marched across it into Hanoi after their resounding success at Dien Bien Phu.

Doumer Bridge was critical to the North's military operations during the American war. Heavily defended by antiaircraft artillery and Soviet SA-2s, the highway and rail span linked Hanoi with its supply route from the Chinese border. Successive waves of U.S. planes tried to bomb it to smithereens, but the bridge was cobbled back into service every time.

We started bombing the North after the infamous Gulf of Tonkin incident, an alleged provocation that has since been disproved. In the summer of 1964 the Seventh Fleet was actively patrolling the gulf, giving radar support to South Vietnamese bombers. One of those ships was the U.S.S. *Maddox*. On the evening of August 4, after spotting two mysterious dots on their radar screen, personnel aboard the *Maddox* signaled that they were under attack by enemy torpedo boats. The following day they corrected the false alarm, attributing their jitters to "freak weather conditions and overeager sonar men," but the die had been cast.

Two months before the spurious attack, President Johnson and Defense Secretary Robert McNamara had ordered a draft version of a U.S. response to North Vietnamese aggression. Swept along by the hysteria that greeted reports of an unprovoked attack on the Seventh Fleet (the correction got lost in the shuffle), on August 7 both houses of Congress overwhelmingly passed the Gulf of Tonkin Resolution, giving the commander in chief full powers to conduct a land, sea, and air war against North Vietnam. Nearly every elected repre-

sentative caved in, including Senator Fulbright, who shep-
herded the vote through the upper house to his everlasting
regret. There were two lone nays in the Senate, Gruening
and Morse.

Shortly after his 1965 inauguration, Johnson ordered
Operation Rolling Thunder, a program of escalated bombings
to cripple the North's rail lines and interdict supply convoys
coming down from the Chinese border. In June 1966 the
bombings were expanded to include massive raids on oil stor-
age depots, power plants, factories, rail yards, and bridges in
the vicinity of heavily populated Hanoi and Haiphong. In
August 1967 Doumer Bridge was hit for the first time; the
rebuilt span was struck again by sorties in October and
December, and again in the early months of 1968. Johnson
delighted in picking the targets himself, in consultation with
his Joint Chiefs, in a basement war room in the White
House.

Over a period of three years and nine months from the
first handful of strikes, there were seven escalating phases to
Operation Rolling Thunder, punctuated by seven halts.
Johnson sanctimoniously announced each halt as his induce-
ment to Hanoi to begin negotiations. Each resumption was
his wrathful punishment after Hanoi failed to knuckle under.
"And so, my fellow Americans, tonight I have ordered . . . "
In all, 643,000 tons of bombs were dropped on the North.
The bombings, more than any other phase of the war, led to
LBJ's downfall. Facing an insurrection within his party—the
"Dump Johnson" movement and the candidacies of Eugene
McCarthy and Robert Kennedy in 1968—he chose not to
seek reelection. In one of the final acts of his presidency, he
discontinued the raids a few days before the November elec-
tions, too late to help Hubert Humphrey.

Historians agree that the bombings had a negligible effect

on the war in the South while they succeeded in stiffening the North's resolve. They also left numbers of downed aviators in North Vietnamese hands, to languish in the Hanoi Hilton, to be paraded through the streets, to become, whatever their private emotions, gaunt, zombielike symbols of America's shame, and valuable pawns for Hanoi in the 1973 Paris peace negotiations that led to the U.S. pullout.

President Nixon resumed the bombings in 1972, along with the mining of Haiphong harbor, turning to football lingo for the code name Linebacker. Precision-guided missiles purportedly capable of surgical strikes rained down on Hanoi and Haiphong. During a wave of Christmas bombings, one of the heaviest inundations of the war, more than two thousand Hanoi civilians were killed. Doumer Bridge was knocked down again. Bach Mai, Hanoi's largest hospital, took a direct hit that had been intended for a nearby helicopter field. The teaching hospital's dermatology staff, as well as its cardiology unit, was wiped out. Bach Mai became yet another rallying point around the world for the antiwar movement.

Going through customs at the airport, I'd fallen in line behind a team of American dermatologists heading for Bach Mai on a goodwill mission. The loss of its top dermatologists, the American doctors told me, was still being felt in a tropical country where fungal infections and skin sores are endemic.

Hanoi's narrow-gauge railway line confused me. I didn't understand why it ran at ground level through a lively residential district near Lenin Park, like a Toonerville Trolley, with only a movable barrier and a few policemen to shoo pedestrians, food carts, notions stalls, and bicycle traffic off the tracks and out of harm's way while a train chugged through. I happened to be standing near the tracks at train time, so I scurried with the crowd and watched from a safe perch. Seconds after the commotion, the carts and stalls reappeared in their original places. Laying a single-line railway through the middle of a populous neighborhood seemed like peculiar city planning, until I realized that the neighborhood had sprung up beside the tracks to accommodate Hanoi's urban sprawl. Lenin Park itself had been a city dump before 1960.

Inside the park, Hanoi's largest stretch of green, I had my first encounter with a familiar sight throughout Vietnam: a configuration of hardware left over from the war and hauled to a popular location to Tell the Story. I never grew totally accustomed to seeing planes, tanks, helicopters, and all the etceteras displayed in museum courtyards and outdoor recreation spots, although there did come a time when I could reel their names off in cozy familiarity: "Oh, right, there's the Phantom, the SAM, and the Huey."

Lenin Park was heavy on Soviet weapons. Nine antiaircraft guns were trained on the twisted fuselage and tail of a B-52. I counted an SA-2 surface-to-air missile on its launcher, a MIG-21, an armored truck, and an early warning radar unit.

Only a few years ago the Museum of Modern Art in New York mounted an exhibition of antiwar imagery by American artists. Some of them had constructed their pieces out of *faux* wreckage, blinking lights, audiotapes, and beeping TV screens. The noisy show was designed to jangle the nerves. I was strangely untouched. Here I was facing the real thing, shrouded in silence. It was powerful art.

"Advanced technology," Mr. Kha surprised me by saying, practically spitting the words. "Vietnam was the arena for the United States and the Soviet Union to test their new weapons."

Had it come down to that ultimately—a war game between two superpowers? Perhaps it had, for recent world events have made a mockery of passionate ideological distinctions. Communism has fallen of its own weight in most places, Russia and China are embracing capitalist economics as fast as they can, Vietnam is endorsing a market economy, and the bottom line for its people had been nationalism all along. Why hadn't we simply let them go their own way? Oh yes, the domino theory. What a joke today, when no one is playing with those dominoes any longer.

My reverie was interrupted by some teenagers hell-bent on practicing their English. "Hell-o. How are *you?*"

Of the many lakes and parks that give Hanoi its restful grace, the enchanting tree-lined ellipse that is Hoan Kiem Lake, in the heart of the city, draws the local population to its neatly tended pathways from dawn, when exercise stalwarts are out in force before reporting to work, until long past sundown, when soft arc lights are reflected in the water and lovers find solitude on discreet stone benches.

The legend of Hoan Kiem Lake takes many forms, all concerning the fifteenth-century warrior king Le Loi and a magic sword loaned to him by a turtle who inhabited the lake bottom. After Le Loi routed the occupying Chinese army, to establish the longest dynasty in Vietnamese history, the turtle reappropriated the sword for safekeeping.

Next to Ho Chi Minh, Le Loi is the most revered patriot of Vietnamese independence. Streets named after him and the village of his birth appear in every city, for with or without a magic sword, the repulsion of Chinese invaders is the central thread in Vietnamese history. Fear of a permanent Chinese occupation after World War II led Ho Chi Minh to make a deal with the weakened French colonialists, and to offer the most pungent rationale ever articulated by a national leader: "Better to sniff a bit of French shit for a few years than to eat Chinese shit for the next thousand years."

The edge of the lake is a block's walk from the Metropole and the official start of our earnest sightseeing with Mr. Kha, although at his urging we'd paid it a visit the night before, assured that it was perfectly safe at all hours. This morning, as we approach the lake, a ring of jovial observers six deep is staring into the water.

"What happened, Mr. Kha?"

"The turtle!" he exclaims. "He comes to the surface once a year. It means good luck."

"Not the original turtle of the legend?"

"A very old turtle. Maybe four hundred years old."

"Really? One turtle in the entire lake?"

"Maybe several turtles. We are very lucky," he says with a happy chuckle. "Last year he didn't show."

"I don't see him. Where is he?"

"There! You can see his head."

"I see him! He's blowing water!"

"He's swimming this way!"

"Look, Maggie, the turtle!"

This is a true story. I saw the turtle. And this is another true story. A few years ago, when the end of the trade embargo seemed in sight, a vice president of the American Express Foundation visited Hanoi with about fifty thousand dollars to spend on a noncontroversial, strictly cultural good-will gesture, to lay the groundwork for introduction of the Card. Of three projects Hanoi's city officials proposed for her consideration, one concerned the turtles at the bottom of Hoan Kiem Lake. Was it possible, they inquired, for American technology to come up with a sonic device that would prod the turtles to surface on cue? She didn't think so, and the discussion turned to more feasible pursuits, like a portico to cover the exposed steles at the Temple of Literature, where the names of the old baccalaureates are inscribed.

I returned to Hoan Kiem Lake twice more on my own, for the upside of jet lag is that if you bound out of bed at an unlikely hour, your unnatural alertness can be put to good advantage. Dressed and raring to go in a sweatshirt and down vest one nippy morning before 6:00 a.m., I strode to the park in the semidarkness, feeling brave and self-conscious.

It was like entering a vast outdoor gymnasium for athletes of all ages and disciplines. Small contingents of women and men were marching in unison down winding footpaths, batting a shuttlecock, tossing a soccer ball. A few individuals were jogging, some had commanded a couple of square feet of space to practice their solitary, elaborate katas, and some were simply limbering up as they walked at a brisk clip, going through the motions of upper-body calisthenics. I fell into formation in the rear row of a class in basic tai chi.

A veteran of many exercise systems, I had no trouble, in principle, following the instructor's *mot, hai, ba, bon* (one, two, three, four), except that I was wackily out of kilter with my classmates, extending my left leg when I should have been extending my right. In fairness to my reputation for agility and coordination, I'd been trained at the New York Health and Racquet Club, and other exercise studios too numerous to mention, to follow the instructor with mirror movements, while at Hoan Kiem Lake in Hanoi, they seemed to do the reverse. Facial isometrics and accompanying grunts were also a challenge, but I felt I'd acquitted myself admirably, and left invigorated after the half-hour drill.

Two mornings later I was back in the park, brimming with confidence. A pale full moon was high in the sky. This time I found an all-women's class that quickly made room for me.

Mot, hai, ba, bon, more missteps and flailing arms in the wrong direction, shy glances and gentle laughter from my classmates. The drill was over too soon. With animated chatter and a firm tug on the arm, I was directed to take my place in a double line and marched to a new location. The sun was full up now. Someone handed me a badminton racquet. Oh, okay. I did miserably with the shuttlecock, swatting it erratically, missing it altogether, almost forgetting in my mortification that the idea was to keep the thing aloft and in play. I sensed that my partner felt embarrassed for me.

The women's idea, however, had been to keep me in tow. One of them had run to get her English-speaking daughter, who arrived on her bicycle, out of breath and sharply dressed. My tai chi classmates gathered round.

"My mother says you joined the class for old women!"

"Tell her I'm not so young myself."

"They want to know where you are from."

"America. New York."

"They want to know, are there classes like this in America?"

"Not in the parks. Not free classes." Ah, tell them what they want to hear. I warmed to the task. "In America we have many exercise classes, and people who wear very fancy exercise clothes, and there are private instructors who come to the homes of the rich, but it's all *very expensive.*"

The women buzzed among themselves, nodding with civic pride.

"They want to know, do you like Hanoi?"

"Tell them I like Hanoi very much. Hanoi is a beautiful city, with beautiful parks. Tell them—" What was it I wanted to tell them? "Tell them . . . " Oh Jesus, god. "Tell them I'm very sorry for what my country did to your country."

And I burst into tears.

My response was a tad more intense than any of us had anticipated. Complex emotions flickered in their eyes, doubtless having to do, in part, with my appalling loss of control.

Setting her chin a little higher, the daughter met my stricken gaze. "They understand."

What could I do except beat a hasty retreat? I wasn't going to stand there bawling, a public water fountain at Hoan Kiem Lake.

There were moments, perhaps that same day, when cynicism became my dominant emotion, in response to what I perceived as cynical behavior on the other end. The first time I saw Ho Chi Minh's picture in Hanoi was on a t-shirt being hawked by a young woman with a hard face who materialized outside a museum just as we arrived. She was tricked out in an olive-green army helmet that was also for sale. If there was a definable tourist market in 1992 for army helmets and Ho t-shirts made on location (true believers? souvenir hunters? collectors of radical kitsch?) I wasn't it.

When it became evident that a sale would not be forthcoming, the woman and her companions eyed me coldly. To them I was that infuriating frustration, a Western tourist who refuses to part with a couple of dollars. I think my strong negative response came from an old allergy to those maddening radicals of political certainty in the sixties who wore Mao, Che, Ho, and (yes, I remember this) "Madame Binh, Live Like Her" across their chests with an in-your-face swagger. Where are those radicals now? Still so certain? I don't know anyone in the nineties who would presume to announce a political world view on his or her chest. My god, in New York people were even shy about putting on a Clinton button in the last days of the campaign, such is our level of political wariness and disbelief in the promises of leaders.

As the war in Vietnam continued to escalate in the late sixties, an angry tremor swept through the peace demonstrations. "End the War Now" and "Bring Our Boys Home" gave way to bands of young militants chanting "Ho, Ho, Ho Chi Minh" as they barreled to the front of the line waving blue, red, and gold Viet Cong flags. At first the mounting anger made me tremble. *Don't do this*, I silently pleaded, we'll all be struck dead by the unforgiving gods of patriotism who demand that we support our country, right or wrong. It was one thing to exercise our democratic right to protest America's military involvement in a tiny, poor Southeast Asian country while yahoos on the sidelines shouted, "Go back to Russia!" It was something else altogether to cheer for the other side.

Or was it? A Communist victory was just what the hardliners warned us would happen unless they increased our troop strength and stepped up the bombing. My objection to the American presence in Vietnam, which got me into the streets marching, wasn't that the war was unwinnable. My objection was that our participation was ill-conceived to begin with, and morally wrong. I agreed wholeheartedly with Dean Rusk, Robert McNamara, William Westmoreland, and Lyndon Johnson that the Communists would win pretty speedily in the South if we pulled out. Like many other Americans deeply disaffected from our nation's foreign policy, ultimately I began to long for that day.

And now, less than twenty-five years after Ho's death, I found disaffected youths in Hanoi peddling Ho t-shirts not from ideological passion but for crumbs of hard currency. The casual debasement made me mourn the blood and the pain of all those of political certainty who fought and died in Vietnam.

Perhaps I was tougher on the t-shirt peddlers than I ought

to have been. Unemployment in Vietnam has hit young people the hardest. Seventy percent of the three and a half million urban jobless are unskilled young workers. Youth are disproportionately represented among the five million who lack jobs in the countryside. And very few young people care to join the Communist Party, whose membership has declined precipitously in recent years.

I still bear Ho, the man, genuine admiration. Of all the heroes in the Marxist pantheon, he still seems the purest—frail of body, canny of mind, ascetic by nature, a revolutionary of perhaps twenty aliases and one overriding vision who devoted his life, thirty years in exile, to writing, exhortation, organizing, clandestine missions, adroit machinations, failed diplomacy, and finally armed struggle in the cause of Vietnamese independence, and who died before the economic theories he attached to his dream proved unworkable for his people.

Whatever it is about the Vietnamese that gives them such resilience, pragmatism, and staying power, such audacious, unswerving focus, it was embodied in the itinerant teacher and restless wanderer from central Vietnam born Nguyen Sinh Cung in 1890. Hopping a freighter in 1911, he set out to work his way around the world—a few months in Brooklyn at the navy yards, assistant pastry chef under Escoffier at the Carlton Hotel in London—before he settled in the Vietnamese expatriate community in Paris. Clever with his hands, he opened a studio for portrait photography and retouching, and began writing for obscure leftist publications under the pseudonym Nguyen Ai Quoc—Nguyen the Patriot. The revolution taking place in Russia kindled sparks in his nationalist soul. He joined the French Communist Party, contributing occasional pieces to *L'Humanité*, speaking at conferences as "the delegate from Indochina."

Colleagues in Paris were impressed by the frugal, celibate ways of the reed-thin Vietnamese with his ill-fitting European suit and disconcerting habit of slipping into a room unnoticed. He had a whimsical sense of humor, a thirst for museums, plays, and concerts, an endearing manner of bestowing impulsive hugs and shy pecks on the cheek. His glowing smile revealed a poor set of teeth; he spoke in a way that suggested he was fighting a slight lisp.

Vietnamese independence was a back-burner concern to French Communists struggling to identify their own working-class issues while paying heed, or lip service, to various anticolonial factions among the political exiles in Paris—Algerians, Syrians, Madagascans, Senegalese, Indians—all clamoring for attention. The French secret police, on the other hand, were taking no chances. They opened a file on Nguyen Ai Quoc and his activities.

In 1924, after six years in Paris, he traveled to Moscow to see the Soviet revolution firsthand, taking classes at an institute for Asian insurgents. Then it was on to Canton, Shanghai, Bangkok, Hong Kong, to found the Indochina Communist Party in 1929. In Hong Kong, sick and tubercular, he was captured and put in a prison hospital, from which he managed an artful escape. With premature sighs of relief the police in Paris closed their file on Nguyen Ai Quoc with the notation "Died in a Hong Kong jail." Prudently abandoning his popular alias, he continued to wander by rail and freighter during the 1930s, sometimes making arduous overland treks, and hooking up briefly with the Chinese Communists at their mountain base in Yenan.

Flushed by their early successes in World War II, the Japanese poured down from China into Vietnam in 1940, to crush and replace the French colonial administration. The following year, disguised as a Chinese journalist in a European suit and soft felt hat, Ho slipped back into his country for the first time in three decades. He was past fifty, weakened from bouts with tuberculosis, malaria, and dysentery. At a northern mountain hideout he met up with two men who were to become his closest comrades, Vo Nguyen Giap and Pham Van Dong, revolutionaries of a younger generation who'd been inspired by his writings and legend. By then he'd adopted his most famous alias, Ho Chi Minh, Bearer of Light. Slipping back into China, he was arrested again, this time by the Kuomintang. In shackles for fifteen months before his release, he managed to compose a short volume of metaphorical poems in classical Chinese.

To the compatriots he rejoined in the mountain caves, he was a revered elder statesman. It was they who began calling him Uncle, or Bac Ho. American intelligence agents in Indochina also took a liking to him; he returned the compliment by developing a taste for American cigarettes. Those were the illusory halcyon days of American-Vietnamese cooperation, when it seemed that the United States might be sympathetic to the nationalist aims of the Viet Minh insurgents. It was not to be. After the Japanese surrender, the U.S. and British allies worked in concert to ease the return of the French colonial administration. By 1954 American flyers were airlifting supplies to the embattled French troops at Dien Bien Phu. The same year, after the Geneva Conference partitioned Vietnam until the lower half of the country could hold elections, the United States began in earnest to prop up the South, inaugurating the second and bloodiest stage of the modern Vietnamese war for independence. Ho did not live to see the day when his country was reunited.

I had already made a decision not to visit his mausoleum. I cringed at the idea of viewing an embalmed body, and I strongly doubted that Ho would have approved either. The frail bachelor head of state who'd received visiting dignitaries in his last years dressed as a peasant, bare-legged in shorts, with sandals cut from old rubber tires (the demonstration of agrarian solidarity appeared unintentionally bohemian), hadn't wished to be embalmed for perpetuity, enclosed under glass in a gargantuan bombproof structure. He'd wanted to be cremated, but his say in the matter had been countermanded by the Party leadership collective, thinking of Lenin in Moscow, and convinced that Ho's surrogate nephews and nieces needed a tangible *something* to worship. Given the bones of saints, bits of hair, and other sacred relics in shrines around the world, not to mention the strong Vietnamese tradition of ancestor worship, they may have been right.

But I had no need to pay final respects as a form of emotional catharsis; nor was I a sightseer driven by ghoulish curiosity. I found no good reason to file past his coffin and peek at the waxen corpse, the wispy beard, the parchment skin.

As it happened, the mausoleum was closed temporarily for repairs.

The yellow, high-walled Hanoi Hilton, which I craned my neck to see on several drive-bys, was about to be torn down. Giving mute testimony to its past and present use as a city prison, the rooftop bristled with jagged glass and electrified barbed wire, and the few windows were heavily barred. After rumors swept the city like a monsoon, it had been confirmed in the local press that Singapore interests had signed a deal to demolish the block-long site and construct Hanoi's first modern office building, which no doubt would be given an innocuous name. News of the joint venture had not been received with warmth in all quarters. The French had used the Hoa Lo stockade to imprison Vietnamese revolutionaries during the colonial wars. It was a desecration, some argued with emotion, to replace the proud historic building with a glass-and-steel monument to capitalist enterprise. Others, attempting to grapple with thorny new environmental issues, raised the question of zoning laws, or rather the lack of them. At twenty stories the proposed tower would dominate the horizon in a city where six stories is high.

On one of our drive-bys, Mr. Kha allows that he's familiar with the inside of the Hanoi Hilton. While a student, he says, he was encouraged to practice his English with those POWs who welcomed the harmless diversion. Wistfully he mentions a particular captain with whom he believes he achieved a friendship.

"But when I tried a few years ago to send my regards through a returning veteran," Mr. Kha says sadly, "I received word that the captain wishes to forget his time in our city."

"Well, Mr. Kha," I say after a pause, "I can certainly see it from his point of view."

Point of view. A poster for *Dien Bien Phu*, the movie, caught my eye outside a local theater. Now, that was something I'd have spent a wad of dong to see, if only to witness the audience reaction. When Mr. Kha inquired about tickets, he found that the movie wasn't playing. It had premiered in Hanoi for an audience of invited guests as part of an international publicity extravaganza staged by the French filmmaker Pierre Schoendoerffer, but it had not gone into general release either in the States or Vietnam. On the whole that may have been just as well, for this third entry of the year in France's cinematic Vietnam sweepstakes (the other two films were *The Lover* and *Indochine*) reenacts the decisive French military defeat from the French point of view.

The maudlin reclaiming by the French of their obsessive,

sentimental, unrequited, sadomasochistic romance with Vietnam is replete with ironies for an American. Drawn as we are as a nation to the Rambo genre of filmmaking that updates Cowboys and Indians to the venue of Southeast Asia, we too fail to approach that critical point of empathy where we can cheer for the Indians.

I mean the Vietnamese. The fortifications held by the French on a remote plain northwest of Hanoi near the Laotian border were considered impregnable, an assumption that critically underestimated the Vietnamese determination to throw off their colonial masters, and the Herculean efforts they would undertake to achieve their goal, guided by the military genius of General Vo Nguyen Giap, one of the great master strategists of all time.

Amid aerial surveillance and bombardment during the fall and winter of 1953, General Giap mobilized his troops to hack trails and dig in, gradually encircling the French encampment with several hundred miles of camouflaged tunnels and trenches. Truck convoys drove by night or in fog without headlights. A rear army of tens of thousands of porters, employing hundreds of sampans and thousands of Iron Horses, French-built bikes modified to carry heavy packs, moved artillery, rice, and ammunition through rivers, mountains, and forests. While fighting diversionary battles elsewhere.

For Giap and the Vietnamese, Dien Bien Phu was like a giant board game of Go, where the intent is to divert and encircle, and then to annihilate once the trap has been laid. The French had two airstrips in their valley, and more than thirteen thousand men, half of them crack paratroopers and Foreign Legionnaires, who were supplied with a stock of wine and two mobile brothels on wheels to keep them contented. On March 13, 1954, the Viet Minh launched a full-scale

offensive. The battle of Dien Bien Phu was a thrilling testament to willpower and human endeavor, on a par with
Waterloo and the battle for Stalingrad. I think we will never
come to terms with Vietnam until we see the fifty-five-day
siege and rout, and the amazing months of preparation that
made it possible, as a Vietnamese triumph, not as a French
defeat.

When it was over, France was finished as a colonial power
in Vietnam and America slipped in to take up the slack.

The 1954 Geneva accords splitting Vietnam in two at the
seventeenth parallel were supposed to be a temporary mea-
sure until the South could hold elections. That October, the
first Viet Minh soldiers walked across the Paul Doumer
Bridge into Hanoi. A pious Catholic protégé of Cardinal
Spellman, Ngo Dinh Diem, billed as "a miracle man," was
installed in Saigon. Without missing a beat, U.S. counterinsurgency teams began destabilizing the North, sowing fear in
an already nervous Catholic minority by proclaiming through
leaflets and loudspeakers that the Virgin Mary was fleeing
south and wished them to join her. During a three-hundred-
day interregnum, more than one million Catholics responded
to the Virgin's call; thousands were evacuated by U.S. transport ships. The lines had hardened. Intent on making South
Vietnam a bulwark of Asian anti-Communism on the model
of South Korea, American foreign policy moved inexorably
and shamefully in the following decade from Eisenhower's
dirty tricks to Kennedy's Green Berets to Lyndon Johnson's
full-scale war.

Point of view, Take 2. Of all the museums I visited in
Hanoi, I was most enlightened by the Fine Arts, a museum
with a major identity problem that turned out to be revela-
tory.

"Fine art" is a hallowed Western European concept rooted in snobbery and defined at its most basic as art that is definitely not practical, useful, or applied decoratively to something that has a utilitarian function, like a pot, a bowl, a chair, a paneled screen, or even a religious icon, if one is a strict purist. It is art for art's sake, created, at least originally, for the pure esthetic enjoyment of aristocratic patrons who could afford to commission and buy the work. A framed painting on canvas exemplifies the definition of fine art. Woodblock prints and lacquered boxes usually don't; although they may have purely decorative value, they fall into the category of artisan crafts.

Fine art, however, is a slippery term. It loses meaning when we explore the ruling esthetics of Eastern traditions, of deeply artistic cultures that didn't paint with oils on canvas or make sculptures from blocks of marble. Adding to the confusion, there have been moments in history when the definition of fine art was deliberately exploded, most vividly after the Russian Revolution, when artists undertook a mission to educate and propagandize, producing Soviet socialist realism. Fine art or not fine art? The debate is not over.

"Skip it," an experienced traveler had said when I'd mentioned Hanoi's Fine Arts Museum. "It's all derivative."

"Go to the Fine Arts. You'll get a great overview of their local handicrafts," advised another traveler, who'd been on a Vietnamese-American Reconciliation Tour.

From the *Lonely Planet* guidebook, an exhaustive, user-friendly tome produced in Australia, I learned that the museum was housed in an old colonial building that used to be the French Ministry of Information. One current highlight, according to the guidebook, was "an incredibly intricate embroidery of Ho Chi Minh reading."

Armed with these tips, I had pretty much eliminated the

Fine Arts from my must-see list until I spoke with an assistant curator at the Freer and Sackler Galleries in Washington, a professional in the field of Asian art who had toured the museum with selective eyes, and who showed me how to decode its contents.

I arrived at the stately building, traversed the folk arts, and climbed to the second floor. There they were! Watercolors, pastels, and oils from the 1930s and 1940s, executed during French colonial rule in the French impressionist manner— the poignant, dutiful, charming results of the *mission civilisatrice* in Indochina. I walked through a roomful of Vietnamese Cézannes, canvas after canvas of romantic, hazy, pastoral visions of calm, sleepy villages and virgin forests in the languorous tropics. Moving to an adjoining room, I found some Vietnamese Mary Cassats, well-to-do, thoroughly Europeanized ladies posing among the comforts of home in cool summer frocks with their perfectly groomed children.

Down on the first floor, the museum's style and contents underwent a sea change. Here were the large, strident oils from the 1960s and 1970s, the Vietnamese adaptations, under Soviet patronage, to the artistic credo of socialist realism. Sturdy, heroic peasants laboring in the fields. Sturdy, heroic soldiers moving forward in battle, hauling heavy artillery up a mountain. Now and again, on both floors, luminous touches of gold lacquer, a traditional Viet technique that I'm as reluctant as they are to say came from China, highlighted the paintings with a lyrical, otherworldly effect.

So how do you adjudicate the fine arts debate when the overriding influence, in every decade, is cultural imperialism? The exhibition had been put together in consultation with a Czech adviser, who, I believe, knew precisely what he was doing.

On an outing to a flower village near West Lake, where

backyard gardeners cultivate seasonal blooms for the market, we stopped off to visit the studio of two young contemporary painters, friends of Barbara Cohen's. The rickety wood house was off a dirt road in a suburban district that appeared distinctly upscale, to judge by the number of refurbished villas. It had been acquired by one of the artists through a family inheritance. I had assumed, incorrectly, that there was no such thing as a privately owned dwelling in Vietnam.

We sat on the floor, on banana-leaf mats, drinking tea and nibbling imported Chinese coconut cookies, making chitchat while Mr. Kha and Phuong Anh did the translating chores. One of the young men, the inheritor of the house, had a job doing restoration work at pagodas and temples. The other taught a class in sketching and experimented on his own time with the application of gold lacquer to his surrealist, semi-abstract versions of Salvador Dali.

Surrounded by paint jars, brushes, stacks of canvases and drawings, I could have been in a struggling artist's studio anywhere, except that I happened to be in suburban Hanoi. I liked the young men and was grateful for their hospitality. I murmured appropriate compliments about their paintings while they inquired about current art trends in New York and wondered if there might be a market for their work.

Hanoi had officially designated orphans, kids with typed badges pinned to their shirts who hung out around Hoan Kiem Lake hawking discarded newspapers and magazines. They were the first beggars I saw in Vietnam, but hardly the last. The farther south I traveled, the more I ran into this Third World fact of life, but only in earnest, proper Hanoi did the kids wear badges, and only in Hanoi were they still so innocent at their trade that they melted away after one firm "No!" When a child at Hoan Kiem approached me with an

English-Vietnamese pocket phrase book, I happily bought it for the satisfactory price, to both sides, of one dollar.

I stuck *Vietnamese So Easy as A.B.C.* into my pants pocket along with a pair of reading glasses. After memorizing *cam on*, "thank you," and adjusting it to "cam-un" to reflect local speech, I saw that pronouncing Vietnamese words aloud would not be a snap just because the basic alphabet looked familiar.

Spoken Vietnamese is a six-tone monosyllabic Mon-Khmer language with borrowings from Thai and Chinese. It is written today in *quoc ngu*, roman letters that are more or less phonetic when they are read with various accent marks and symbols. Carats, slashes, curlicues, dots, and squiggles identify the tones: rising, falling, level, low rising, falling and rising, and low glottalized stop. Reading without these pronunciation aids, one would have to wonder why so many short words seem to carry so many different meanings.

For the tourist context I was operating in, that didn't present a problem. When I saw *pho* on a street sign, I figured out, eventually, that it meant "street." Seeing *pho* on a restaurant sign, I understood that the establishment served Hanoi's hearty noodle soup with chicken or beef, and that I should pronounce it "fa." Studying the blue shapes on my map, I cleverly deduced that *ho* meant "lake"—not "hole," or "tiger," or "kitty," or "fox," or "cough," or "wine bottle," or "rice water," or the father of Vietnamese independence.

The story of *quoc ngu* (pronounced "kwok noo-oo," with a stop in the falling-and-rising inflection) is another lesson in the Vietnamese ability to adapt, assimilate, and appropriate as needed. Early speakers of Vietnamese did not have a written language before they were conquered by the Chinese empire in 111 B.C. and first appeared in recorded history.

With Chinese control came Chinese education and Chinese ideographs, at least for the mandarin class that administered the realm. The peasants remained illiterate, although they were the repository of a rich oral tradition of poems, legends, and fables. By the fourteenth century a writing system called *nom* had gained adherents among the gentry. It employed Chinese characters phonetically to record Vietnamese folk tales and Buddhist teachings. "In general," writes John DeFrancis in *Colonialism and Language Policy in Viet Nam*, "the same people commanded both of these scripts," and often the two forms were studied together.

In 1624, intent on converting the pagans, a French Jesuit, Alexandre de Rhodes, traveled to Vietnam with religious credentials from Rome and safe-conduct papers from Portugal, whose merchants were the first Europeans to trade in the region. Fearing his sermons would fall on deaf ears, he buckled down and learned the native language, which sounded to him at first like the twittering of birds, especially when spoken by women.

A "bright native boy," whose name he did not record, volunteered to teach the Jesuit father the rising and falling inflections. Rhodes took notes. His early attempts at speech, he wrote in his autobiography, were not without egregious bloopers, like the order he gave his helpers one day to cut down a stand of bamboo saplings, which came out, "Kill the children." Ten years into his mission, he was expelled from the country, his apostolic credentials revoked by Rome after the Portuguese accused him of favoring French interests. By then he had compiled his romanized dictionary, with translations into Latin and Portuguese. It was presented to the Vatican, where it languished as an oddity for the next couple of centuries.

The Rhodes dictionary used letter combinations from several romance languages, plus Latin and Greek, a hint that the Jesuit had borrowed from the phrase books of missionaries who preceded him. Some of the value-for-value substitutions appear arbitrary and old-fashioned today. Written Vietnamese does not have an *f*, *j*, *w*, or *z*, although these consonants are common in the spoken language. The *f*-sound is written as *ph*, from romanized Greek, which also provides *th* and *kh*. The *w*-sound is dispatched in combinations like *oa* and *hu*, or in a *u* that follows a *q*. The letter *d* without a horizontal crossbar is pronounced like a soft French *j* or a hard *z*, depending on what region the speaker hails from or what vowel follows hard on its heels. When *nh* appears at the end of a word, the sound is a faint -*ng*, as in Ho Chi Ming, a pronunciation that surprises most Westerners. At the beginning of a word, *nh* is like the Spanish *n* in *mañana*.

Rhodes and his brethren never expected their script to be anything more than a pony to help them gain converts. In that regard, *quoc ngu* was a great success, helping to produce a substantial minority of Vietnamese Catholics (and paving the way for religious divisiveness down the line). Unaffected by the Rhodes alphabet, Vietnam's mandarin class continued to receive a classical Chinese education, and to write in Chinese under the old Confucian system while employing *nom* in the creation of literary compositions.

When the French seized administrative control of Vietnam in the nineteenth century, they stamped out Chinese and didn't care much for *quoc ngu*, either. First of all, it wasn't French enough for them. Second, they feared it might perpetuate a national identity and a means of communication among a subject people who would be easier to handle, not to mention better off culturally in terms of the *mission civilisatrice*, if they were taught rudimentary French. Used to a bilingual system, many educated Vietnamese agreed. It wasn't until the twentieth century that Vietnamese nationalists endorsed *quoc ngu* wholeheartedly as the sole acceptable written form of their language.

The decision to promote *quoc ngu* was a big step for an independence movement in a little country whose neighbors wrote in ideographs or in derivations of Sanskrit, whose peasants were illiterate, and whose educated elite grew up with Chinese or French as their second language. Ho Chi Minh was among those language reformers who advocated *quoc ngu* even though he railed against aspects of the romanization: the words looked fussy on the page, the letters required special type fonts, they were useless for telegrams. But *quoc ngu* worked for patriotism as it had worked for the catechism. It was easier to read than Chinese characters, it didn't require endless study, and most important, it was unique to Vietnam. The script emerged from obscurity to find a prideful new identity in poems, essays, newspapers, in medical manuals and popular science texts, and in leaflets, banners, and posters calling for revolution.

Immediately after Ho Chi Minh's declaration of independence in 1945, the one that borrowed precepts from America's 1776 declaration ("We hold the truth that all men are created equal," Ho began), the Viet Minh organized patriotic campaigns to eradicate illiteracy, urging rich and poor, young and old, husbands and wives, to teach one another *quoc ngu*. Up to his death, Ho favored a streamlined alphabet, leaving a will that deliberately used *f* for *ph*, and *z* for *d*.

Naturally, I forgot to take the phrase book the day Maggie had us stop for a photo op at a farming village we'd seen from the road. A peasant was driving an oxcart. Piglets scrambled in a sunny dell. The gently sloping hillside only a few miles from Hanoi had an Angelus quality of bucolic peace that sent the photographer into high gear. I got out of the car to join her, and we climbed a narrow dirt path to see what serendipitous treats for her camera lay beyond the rise.

"It's okay to do this?" I asked Mr. Kha.

"Why not?" he shrugged.

The answer, I'd thought, was obvious. Tourists had not been permitted such spontaneous freedom a few years before.

"And the villagers won't mind?" I pressed.

"Ah, you know the famous saying of Ho Chi Minh, 'Nothing is more precious than freedom and independence.' That's what the people are saying they want now, freedom and independence." He beamed at his little joke.

Another misconception about Vietnam was about to be shattered. I'd imagined that farms were organized into big communes, à la the disastrous collective experiments in Russia and China, but my information was behind the times.

Because of its head start during the fifties, the North had suffered the brunt of the mismanaged farm collective movement that was supposed to be the beating heart of Vietnam's socialist economy. Peasants who had welcomed land reform—that is, the appropriation of big landlord holdings—were unpleasantly surprised when the second half of the package, that quintessential Marxist slogan "From each according to his ability, to each according to his need," went into effect.

Instead of a utopian redistribution of wealth, the farmers found they were producing crops at low prices for government collectors who to their mind were becoming suspiciously similar to the old landlords and their hated agents. Left to fill rice quotas without a personal incentive, paddy workers had taken the path of least resistance and simply slacked off. Stuck with a government pricing system that actually fell below their production costs, sugarcane growers reacted to the centralized mismanagement by destroying their canefields to plant other crops.

Reality hit Hanoi's leaders during the middle eighties when Vietnam, a country with two fertile deltas capable of producing three rice crops a year, was forced to become a rice-importing nation for the first time in history (except during the American war). After many agonizing sessions of the Communist Party Central Committee, the profit incentive was reintroduced. By the end of the decade, Vietnam was firmly in place as the third largest rice exporter in the world, behind Thailand and the United States. More changes followed. Recently the National Assembly granted families that tilled small individual holdings (three hectares, or seven and a half acres) twenty-year renewable tenure rights for annual crops, and fifty-year rights on similar-sized spreads growing long-term crops.

As we headed their way, the village children ran to greet us. I guessed they were saying, "My name is . . . what's yours?" or "Hey, where are you from?" I felt oafish and tongue-tied, a trespasser without gifts. The trinkets I'd brought from America for just such an occasion were at the hotel, along with the phrase book.

With Mr. Kha trailing behind, we let the children lead us deeper into the village, down a path to a little cemetery hidden in a glen. Hard by the graveyard there was a wood Buddhist temple with a padlocked door. I walked around it, trying to peer in. "They're getting someone to open it for you," said our guide. There was more to this village than he had expected.

Calm and composed, a female monk in brown robes, her head wrapped in a maroon turban, appeared with a key. With stately grace, she ushered us inside.

While the children watched from the doorway, the monk brewed some tea and put out a plate of sweets and bananas. Smiling beatifically, she told us through Mr. Kha that she was forty-two years old and had been at the village for three years. She depended on the farmers for her food and lodgings, as was the Buddhist way. We admired the array of cheap gilt Buddhas on her altar. We ate a banana, we sipped tea. Maggie asked if she could take some pictures.

"Is that usual, Mr. Kha? A female monk?" I inquired.

"Ah, yes. Sometimes," he whispered conspiratorially. "They are women disappointed in love."

A knowledge of Buddhism was not one of Mr. Kha's strong points. Unlike the neighboring Cambodians, Vietnamese Buddhists invited women into their ranks. Dimly I recollected that at least one female monk from Hue had immolated herself during the Buddhist demonstrations of the sixties. Vietnam's political relaxations of the last few years had prompted an astonishing resurgence of Buddhism in the countryside, along with a national craze for lottery tickets and fortune-tellers. Folk festivals geared to the lunar calendar were proliferating all over the place. A village like this one could reopen its temple and hire a monk.

While Maggie photographed our stately cleric, I lolled on a stone bench in the sun, the children vying for a place at my side. Emboldened, they stroked my arm, comparing its color to their forearms and legs. It's a Vietnamese thing, this tactile stroking. A sign of approval. I felt very honored. Rummaging in my purse, I came up with a lone stick of chewing gum and presented it to my favorite, a cross-eyed girl of about ten. No slouch at pantomime, she touched it to her heart.

"*Ciao,*" the children called after us as we made our way back to the road. *Ciao?* Was it possible these kids had been watching Italian movies?

Back at the hotel, I checked my phrase book. *Chao*, an all-purpose word for hello and goodbye.

With *chao* and *cam on*, I sailed through the civilities of subsequent outings, but nothing ever quite matched the dreamlike encounter with the female monk and the children who stroked my arm at the little farm outside Hanoi.

Americans bearing chewing gum and trinkets are an established tradition wherever a jet or a cruise ship can take us. But since this is Vietnam, a piece of gum or candy seems to carry a special freight.

Choose the single most frightful image that turned you against the war. The naked girl running down the highway, her back and shoulders scorched from napalm?

The tag line from a Mike Wallace interview after My Lai, reproduced on a poster?

"And babies?"

"And babies."

While their parents hold back, inquisitive children are always the first to reach out to strangers. GIs below the seventeenth parallel often befriended the tykes who hung around base camps or sidled up to them on patrols, hoping for a can of C-rations or candy. But sometimes bored, scared GIs made paranoid-crazy by the war played darker games with Vietnamese children. Tossing candy into concertina wire to watch them scramble. Hurling full cans of C-rations at their heads from a moving truck. As reported by the participants, these responses appear in the Winter Soldier Investigation conducted by Vietnam Veterans Against the War.

At the height of the war, the writer Grace Paley and some of her friends began holding a silent Saturday afternoon vigil at the triangle between the traffic lanes on Sixth Avenue in

Greenwich Village. They held up posters saying "Not Our Sons, Not Their Sons." Calling themselves Mothers for Peace, they kept at it for years, rain or shine.

Coincidentally, the first Vietnamese restaurant to try its luck in New York after the war was located on Sheridan Square a few blocks from the site of that silent vigil. In a bow to neighborhood trends—a Szechuan Village and a Hunan Village within shouting distance—the owners called it Vietnam Village. I used to pass Vietnam Village on my way to the bank. The name gave me the shivers—concertina wire, strategic hamlets, GIs torching thatched roofs with Zippo lighters. In a matter of months the restaurant closed for lack of business. I probably wasn't the only neighborhood person who just couldn't make it through the door. A later wave of Vietnamese restaurants, I noticed, took names like Indochine and Cuisine de Saigon that were easier on the emotions.

In Hanoi they eat lunch and dinner early. Six p.m. marks the start of the dinner hour; 11:30 to 12:30 is the usual time for lunch. By noon most days, after a full morning of museums and pagodas, we were as ready as Mr. Kha for the culinary phase of our strenuous research. Maggie and I abandoned our plans to knock off a couple of pounds. Our eager guide knew the best places and gallantly helped us overorder.

Cha ca means grilled fish. We climbed a creaking flight of wood stairs at 14 Cha Ca Street, in the heart of the Old Quarter, and waited for a window table at Cha Ca La Vong, which made its reputation with a secret recipe for curried Red River fish that had been in the family for generations. An accompanying shrimp sauce, smelling like limburger cheese, tested the outer limits of our Western palates.

According to a government booklet, there are five hundred varieties of crab, saltwater and freshwater, in the Socialist Republic of Vietnam. It seemed imperative to pay a return visit to 202 Hue in order to see if the sautéed crabs were as good at lunchtime as at dinner. They were.

Restaurant 75, in a French row house bearing that number on Tran Quoc Toan, created an illusion of Old World charm with modern Vietnamese ceiling fans and Czech chandeliers. To a piped-in tape of easy-listening instrumentals—"Where Have All the Flowers Gone?" and "Buttons and Bows"—we feasted on spring rolls, crab soup, stuffed crab, and sizzling, spicy fish with tomato sauce and sautéed greens. The kitchen help came out to look us over when they heard our American voices. Restaurant 75 had a prosperous-looking clientele; they turned out to be executives from a Japanese trading company.

Slowly it dawned on us that most of the Asian faces we were seeing in Hanoi's upscale restaurants weren't Vietnamese. Local folk usually grabbed a bite at an outdoor stall or a "dusty rice" noodle shop for forty or fifty cents. (The Vietnamese love to speak in metaphors. "Dusty rice" is the general term for street food. "Dust-of-life" refers to society's victims—orphans, vagrants, addicts, amputees, and the like.)

On our fancy restaurant circuit, the bills seldom came to more than twenty dollars for four, including a round of joint-venture beer and Coca-Cola imported from Taiwan. Relatively expensive items, the Cokes were for me and the drivers, who changed every day. Shy youths who seemed to have been chosen for their probity as much as for their mechanical skills, they weren't permitted to drink beer on the job. They hankered for the American beverage and all it stood for, but they'd never presume to order a can unless they saw me order one first. As the ranking elder, I was expected to provide certain social cues. I ended up drinking a lot of Coke in Vietnam.

The two basic ways a tourist absorbs a foreign culture are through buying and eating. When I traveled through China in 1977, I had to admit that I'd eaten better Chinese food in New York. The few Vietnamese restaurants I'd tried at home had served delectable spring rolls, but the rest of the meal had not been transporting. Thailand was the first foreign country I visited that had inspired me to say, "You have no idea how good the food is until you go there."

And now Vietnam. Why should that be? For one thing, few of the country's great chefs have migrated elsewhere. For another, some indigenous spices and staple ingredients, such as lemon grass, fresh coconut milk, and *nuoc mam*, a fermented anchovy sauce that is the national condiment, aren't readily available in other parts of the world.

An old Vietnamese proverb goes, "Heaven punishes, Heaven reprimands, but Heaven does not punish people when they are eating." Pressed for a cultural stereotype, I'd say that the Vietnamese are a nation of serious, sensual, and prideful eaters. There is a story, possibly apocryphal, about the peasant from one of the poorer provinces who went on a journey with a wooden fish in his pocket. In an eating house, when all he could afford was a bowl of rice and a dish of *nuoc mam*, he'd dip his fish into the sauce and pretend to be savoring a full meal. Trudging along the road again, he'd keep up his spirits by sucking the remaining flavor from the wood.

A diner who appreciates the subtle wonders of Vietnamese cuisine can't help but acquire a gut-level understanding of Vietnamese history. Over the centuries gastronomic contributions from several conquering nations were orchestrated by local cooks into a distinct and original gestalt. Early and frequent invasions by China brought in stir-fry cooking along with bean curd, rice noodles, and chopsticks. A lengthy and honorable Buddhist vegetarian tradition encouraged the inventive use of fresh greens, shoots and sprouts, and contrasting textures. A beef eater's Mongolian hot-pot tradition probably originated during the thirteenth-century invasion by Kublai Khan. In addition to leaving Vietnamese cooks with the culinary secrets of hidden caramelized sauces and crusty baked bread, the French added white potatoes, tomatoes, and asparagus to the vegetable patch and the local cuisine. Seizing upon the humble, ubiquitous banana, they dressed it up for dessert, at least in restaurants catering to Europeans, as bananas flambé. Finally, there's the absolute freshness of the food. This watery land of lakes and rivers bordering the Gulf of Tonkin and the South China Sea is blessed with an abundance of fish and crustaceans.

Chinese gourmets, I learned, were behind another culinary tradition that took hold in the north. I had inadvertently raised Mr. Kha's hopes the first day by announcing that I adored roast duck.

"Dukh? You like dukh?"

"Doesn't everybody like duck?"

"*You have eaten dukh?*" There was a moist gleam in our guide's eye that I couldn't account for.

"Mr. Kha, that's d-u-c-k."

Dog is a winter treat in Hanoi, and the weather had turned chilly. It was a natural misunderstanding.

One rainy afternoon I took shelter in the History Museum, called the Musée Louis Finot when it opened early in the century under the auspices of the Ecole Française d'Extrême-Orient, the umbrella organization for French archeological digs in Indochina. I was the only visitor. Floorboards creaked, the lighting was dim, the descriptions on faded three-by-five index cards in the dusty glass cases were typed in *quoc ngu*. If there were signs saying "Don't Touch," they weren't in English. I touched. The curator looked the other way.

The History Museum is home to artifacts of the mysterious and creative Dong Son civilization, a people also known as Lac Viet, whom modern Vietnamese claim as their direct antecedents. Named for the district in Thanh Hoa province, south of Hanoi, where their pottery and bronzes were first unearthed, the Dong Sons thrived in the Red River Delta and central Vietnam from the fifth to the second centuries B.C. In addition to their activities as seafarers, hunters, and rice growers who kept water buffalo and pigs, the Dong Sons were skilled miners and smelters.

Huge bronze drums, etched on their sides with sun images, deer hunts, fishing boats, and birds, are the most exciting pieces of Dong Son art. They are sometimes called rain drums. The handles, I noticed when I looked more closely, were decorated with tiny sculptures of copulation: frogs on frogs, humans on humans. Eroticism may or may not have been the intent; the drums, I read later, are usually thought to have religious significance. According to Bernard Philippe Groslier in *The Art of Indochina*, they were beaten in sympathetic magic, "in imitation of the thunder which heralded the welcome rain."

The Dong Son civilization lost its spirited originality, and much of its identity, when the Chinese invaded the Red River Delta in the second century B.C. In case a visitor misses the point, a modern mural depicting the watershed Vietnamese uprising against the invaders—the Bach Dang River campaign and victory of A.D. 939—occupies one of the museum's walls.

After I had my fill of the Dong Son bronzes, I moved on to the glass cases displaying Vietnamese pottery from the Ly and Tran dynasties. When Vietnam emerged as an independent kingdom in the tenth century and the royal city of Hanoi was founded, local artisans employed the rich clay of the Red River Delta to produce an inspired range of glazed ceramics. Ly dynasty pots from the eleventh and twelfth centuries have incised painted flowers and leaves in brown glaze on a white background. In Tran dynasty stoneware of the thirteenth and fourteenth centuries, the taste was for monochromatic glazes of white, chocolate brown, or bright apple green. By the fifteenth century, Muslim traders had brought in cobalt from the Middle East, initiating the era of blue-and-white designs at Bat Trang and other kiln centers that continues to this day.

Despite a design repertoire and exuberant brushwork distinctly its own, Vietnam's blue-and-white found its way to the international market in China's shadow, where it still remains. Covered jars and tea sets made for export reflected commercial demands that they *look* Chinese. Foreign merchants wanted "sinification," and the ever adaptable Vietnamese complied.

Firing continuously for five hundred years, the kilns of Bat Trang are a future archeologist's dream. For the present, Vietnamese pottery still suffers from an identity problem. Antique dealers from Bangkok to New York stick to the discredited word "Annamese" (of Chinese origin, it means "of the pacified South") for anything old that was made in Vietnam. New wares based on old designs have lost favor with the local people. Recently, I'd heard, the kilns had been churning out cups and bowls for domestic use stamped "Made in China," appealing to those who still believe that foreign is better.

Flea markets back home had whetted my interest in antiques generally, and a couple of monographs I'd found at the Metropolitan Museum had whetted my interest in Vietnamese ceramics. I yearned to acquire a small old dish, something modest, almost negligible, enhanced by the soft luster of centuries of loving use. Easier said than done. The Vietnamese government might look the other way when a private shopkeeper sold an antique, but customs officials trained by Russian advisers didn't permit antiques to leave the country.

How could I object to a policy whose intent was to preserve what was left of the national heritage? During the war, antiques had been drained from Vietnam—perhaps "looted" is more accurate—by journalists, diplomats, military officers, and others who may not have known what they had but could see it was old and pretty. A sub rosa trade in illegal antiques still flourishes, the valuable items smuggled past airport detectors in risk-free diplomatic pouches.

Well! Perhaps I could buy an illicit souvenir and stuff it among my underthings near the bottom of my suitcase? I tried to tamp down this larcenous impulse and rechannel it into new ceramics that repeated old forms and designs. Present-day kilns weren't on the standard tourist program, but then again, what was the standard tourist program in Vietnam? We were making it up as we went along.

Five of us, plus the driver, crowded into the car for our trip to Bat Trang. Alerted by fax to my interest in the pottery village, Mr. Kha had taken the initiative to scout the five-hundred-year-old complex the week before. Barbara Cohen, who was familiar with Bat Trang ceramics, elected to join us and bring Phuong Anh.

We were champing at the bit as we entered the walled village, a noisy, gritty complex of narrow mud lanes, artisan workshops, treadle wheels, and small cross-draft kilns. Moistened pats of charcoal, straw, and manure, used for fuel, were drying in rows on the brick walls. A woman was stoically mixing and stirring a vat of wet clay with her feet. Moving slowly, with an occasional beep of the horn, our car was a twentieth-century intrusion. A woman hauling a wheelbarrow of clay nearly collided with a dray horse and driver steering a wagonload of finished bowls tied up in bundles of straw. Children scampered by. Vendors hawked slabs of meat and mounds of fruit at a crossroads market. Families sat convivially in their open workshops, eyeing us curiously as they ate lunch among their wares.

"Just let us off anywhere, Mr. Kha," I pleaded.

No such luck. Our guide was determined that we benefit from his advance preparations. The driver circled and recircled the village until Mr. Kha found the lane he was looking for. A young potter who'd been expecting us, apparently, led us into his studio and began his spiel.

Nothing dampens the spirit more than a lecture when the true joy of unscripted discovery lies in wait around the corner. I've been trapped by a drone at the pyramids in Cairo, cornered by a shrill automaton reciting a memorized litany at the Palace of Knossos on Crete. Once, tripping merrily through the Pergamon in East Berlin when there was still a wall, I ran into forty miserable Soviet tourists huddled at the end of a gallery while an East German lecturer held forth with simultaneous Russian translation. The captive Russians glared at me with undisguised hostility. I thought it had something to do with my capitalist clothes. Now I believe it was my freedom to roam at will through beautiful treasures that made them glower.

I assumed an attentive expression while the young master potter of Bat Trang explained that there were two thousand families in his village, and eight hundred kilns, but only thirty families of superior potters, which included him. Feeling like a buyer from Bloomingdale's who has decided not to place an order, I examined his plates and vases, plinking them, turning them upside down. Maggie excused herself to photograph something outside, Barbara and Phuong Anh rushed to carry her tripod. Reduced to an audience of one, the young master potter soldiered on, wrenching the joy from my day in Bat Trang with statistics.

Of all the sins that Soviet advisers perpetrated on their client countries, one of the most heavy-handed was their model for managing tourists. Operating from the premise that foreigners were a disruptive element and needed watching, they devised a conveyor belt that left nothing to chance. Tourist hotels were constructed on the city's outskirts to minimize contacts with local people. Access to a farm or a factory was controlled by people's committees, replacing spontaneous exchanges with canned speeches.

What other model did the Vietnamese have to learn from?

Mr. Kha was beaming at what he had wrought. My companions were roaming free in the village. I picked up a blue-and-white soup tureen awash in peonies, dragonflies, bamboo. It was fitted with a lid and tiny anchovy handles. It was traditional and not traditional. It was lovely.

"How much?"

"This is a demonstration pot that I made," said the potter. "One of a kind."

I braced myself for the tariff that would purchase my freedom.

"Two thousand dong," he said shyly, looking to Mr. Kha for approval. Twenty cents. Mortified once again by the exchange rate, I gave him the money.

With the potter and Mr. Kha at my heels, I ran outside.

"The potter will escort you," Mr. Kha called out.

"Please, no!" I called back.

Barbara and Phuong Anh were around the corner. Like naughty children released from school, we darted in and out of lanes, poking among untended piles of teacups and vases, huge jardinieres, rows of molded ashtrays shaped like lions and frogs and probably destined for export. We climbed onto the veranda of a lordly tiled villa that belonged, no doubt, to a family of superior potters. We ducked into another family's showroom and spied a cache of "copy" antiques in a wood-and-glass cabinet. Surprised by our interest, an unembarrassed workman cheerfully dusted a plate to reveal the imitation fine crackle and emblematic chocolate-colored wash on the underside that clearly were no guarantee of authenticity. For twenty cents a plate, I bought us each a copy antique.

The day will come soon, I hope, when the potters of Bat Trang are visited by real buyers from Bloomingdale's who place gigantic orders for coffee mugs, oven-proof casseroles, open-stock dishes, when archeologists excavate the shards of antiquity that lie buried beneath the mud lanes, and when tourists better mannered than we were pour from their buses to stroll through the village and purchase their own hand-painted blue-and-white pots. And listen to lectures if they want to.

As for me, I carted my twenty-cent soup tureen, my twenty-cent copy antique, and my thirty-cent incense pot from the street stall in Hanoi all over Vietnam. Egged on by a French tourist in Hue, I broke down and bought, for seven dollars, a worn, faded seventy-five-year-old plate (or so the concessionaire estimated) that I seriously doubted would get by customs. Its blue was softer and greyer than the bright cobalt of the stuff from Bat Trang—the distinctive "Hue blue" from that city's pottery works, I learned—and it was as close as I dared come to a genuine antique. I wrapped my Hue plate especially carefully and stuck it among my cheaper treasures. Feeling sentimental when I got to Saigon, I purchased yet another new Bat Trang pot for the grossly inflated price of two dollars. At Tan Son Nhut airport my entire ceramic collection showed up on the X-ray screen like a smuggler's haul and was inspected twice by hand. Nestled among its Bat Trang cousins, the little plate from Hue escaped detection, but somewhere in transit it broke in five pieces. I did a nice job of gluing when I got home.

Home is where I have the patience for statistics that I don't have when I travel. After I returned from Vietnam, I looked up a published paper by Hy Van Luong, a Vietnamese professor of anthropology at the University of Toronto. Professor Luong did field research on Bat Trang's transformation into a state enterprise, a movement born of socialist idealism that peaked in the late 1970s, and the reascendance of private family kilns that took place in the following decade under the *doi moi* reforms. In the early idealist phase of Vietnam's Marxist economics, the government's ambitious policy for the state enterprise at Bat Trang introduced larger, modern kilns, New Year's bonuses, rice subsidies, merit increases, seventeen paid holidays a year, health and retirement plans, paid maternity leaves, a training program for new workers, and a work-study program up to the university level offering two months of paid educational leave each year for qualified employees. Rarely, if ever, was a worker fired. Instead, in a brave attempt to absorb and employ the growing population, the state went out of its way to hire more workers than were actually needed. Bat Trang's state enterprise got first dibs on high-quality clay, pigments, and other raw materials, and its finished ceramics received preferential treatment in distribution and marketing from the state trading company.

The upshot was a socialist disaster. Beset by a series of economic crises related to mismanagement and international pressures, the government grew tardy in its payments. Wages lagged 25 percent behind inflation. Employees did not develop the prideful sense of collective ownership and loyalty that family members had for the family kilns. Instead, they slipped into a dependence mentality and displayed a casual unconcern for the state's property. Absenteeism soared to 30 percent. With its ceramic output guaranteed a market, creativity at the state kiln faltered. At the family kilns, a piece of clay that fell to the floor would be picked up to avoid waste. If it rained at night, the entire family would get up to move the charcoal and firewood to a dry place. At the state enterprise, a bureaucrat would fill out an official form blaming the weather and damp fuel. Surplus inventories of unwanted goods collected at the state kiln. The flexible family kilns made innovative changes and began undercutting the state's prices on the open market.

What happened at Bat Trang turned out to be typical of the majority of state enterprises in Vietnam, where the list of overlapping woes might include inefficiency, overemployment, overcentralization, antiquated equipment, slowness to respond to change, a mind-set intent on filling production quotas determined by the government rather than by consumer demand, overly optimistic financial reports and ultimately dishonest ledger accounts, an entrenched bureaucracy bloated by managers chosen for their past skills in revolution and warfare rather than for their ability to run a corporation, and in some cases, mostly on the provincial or district level, a siphoning off of profits by corrupt officials. Adding insult to injury, the tax burden was heavier, and more collectible, at the state enterprises than at the newly privatized, or reprivatized, operations.

Today Vietnam is divesting itself of its unprofitable state enterprises as fast as it can.

Mr. Kha was late that night getting home to his family. He dropped us off at Barbara's hotel, the Especen Tourism and Cultural Center, a funky establishment overlooking a big courtyard that was used by a martial arts studio. Barbara's room had a bed, a flush toilet, a horizontal pole suspended from the ceiling where she hung her clothes, and just enough space for a desk and her computer. "The people here are my family," she said with an airy wave. "You can always leave a message at the desk for me."

She introduced us to Bob, another Especen resident on an extended visa. Bob was a geologist. "I'm planning a field trip up north," he mysteriously confided, "but Barbara can tell you I'm having a rough time getting permissions."

"To look for what?" I inquired.

"Minerals," he muttered, changing the subject.

After watching the martial arts students perform their katas in the fading light, we hopped into some cyclos and headed for the Metropole.

In the protocol of the bath, the guests get to go first. Barbara took my tub while Phuong Anh went across the hall with Maggie.

"Show her how to use the fixtures," Barbara called out. "Phuong Anh doesn't know about Western bathtubs."

Phuong Anh was a quick study. Maggie gave her a pair of silver earrings to dress up her blouse and jeans. Barbara changed into a lavender *ao dai* on my side of the hall.

Freshly washed and groomed, the four of us sailed into the dining room to gorge on pâté, champagne, and filet mignon, finishing with a round of chocolate mousse and *oeufs à la neige*.

The bill came to slightly under two hundred dollars.

On the mornings when I didn't make it to my exercise class, I took a stroll in the opposite direction from Hoan Kiem Lake, past the gingerbread opera house built by the French in 1911, to an outdoor stall with tiny tables on Ly

Dao Thanh, where a woman and her helpers did a brisk business dishing out *pho*.

Cooked over a brazier, bubbling *pho* is Hanoi's breakfast treat, although it is consumed throughout the day until the pot is empty and the cook closes her stall. A gingery broth of *nuoc mam*, star anise, scallions, coriander, potatoes, onions, chick peas, cinnamon, and garlic is ladled over rice noodles and a hearty portion of beef or chicken. The diner livens the soup with a dash of chili pepper and a squeeze of lime, adding shredded cabbage and bean sprouts from side dishes on the table. It's perfectly good etiquette to wipe your soup spoon and chopsticks with a paper napkin.

For forty cents, the woman on Ly Dao Thanh, blue racing stripes on her Adidas-style track suit, served her *pho* with a wing and a leg of chicken. A boiled egg or fried gizzards cost a few pennies extra. Much as I wanted to throw some fresh greens into my bowl, following the custom of the breakfast club, I denied myself the full range of textures for fear that the greens had been washed in contaminated water. I resolutely stayed phobic about the water in Vietnam, although in time I reduced my vigilance on the greens, to no ill effect.

This sidewalk cafe had a varied clientele that I couldn't stop watching: preoccupied office workers fueling up for the day; an army officer and his girlfriend zooming up noisily on a fancy imported motorcycle; a local toff, dazzling in a checked suit, white tie, gold ring, gold watch, gold tie clasp, and rhinestone lapel pin shaped like a treble clef, who refused to make eye contact; jovial mechanics from the motorcycle shop next door; a proper Japanese tourist and his well-mannered little son.

On my second visit, a man at my table poured some murky brown liquid from a communal bottle into a cup. I followed suit, expecting some kind of tea. It was some kind of rice wine, at 7:30 in the morning. I weaved back to the Metropole to clear my head with a $2.50 cup of coffee.

As rice is the nation's basic food, rice wine is the national inebriant, the Vietnamese version of Japanese *sake*. Before that morning's initiation, I hadn't given any thought to its place in the culture, or to the sociological observation—made by a Frenchman—that the Vietnamese rice field does double duty by provisioning a grateful population with the blessings that a country like France divides between its wheat fields and its vineyards. Ngo Vinh Long, a professor of Vietnamese history at the University of Maine, soberly records that the national importance of rice wine is expressed by the saying "A man without wine is like a flag without wind."

"Vietnamese drink too much," Mr. Kha said primly when I told him about the surprise in my cup that morning. I gathered that national drinking habits had been the subject of much recent public discussion. If foreign brewers enjoy continued success in their efforts to penetrate the Vietnam market, I predict that joint-venture beer will replace the traditional beverage. Halida, a joint venture with Denmark, was Mr. Kha's brew of choice.

At any hour the Metropole's lounge was buzzing with international accents, just what you'd expect at Hanoi's only deluxe hotel. The French tourists had to ask for their coffee and drinks in English, an interesting twist of international fate.

The funniest voices I heard in the lounge belonged to American businessmen making their first tentative approaches to Vietnamese officials. New to Hanoi, uncertain as to exactly whom they were addressing, the Americans spoke unnaturally slowly. "We expect that we'll be able to do some business here soon when the trade embargo is lifted, I mean, when your government, uh, clears up the MIA problem, and uh, it looks, uh, like that is happening." I swear that's what they were saying. They sounded like Americans you hear in foreign movies: nasal, twangy. Their Vietnamese counterparts usually smiled a lot and were noncommittal.

It was going to be heavy sledding for the Americans once they got the green light from our government, as smart, experienced investors from Singapore and Taiwan already knew. They'd be dealing with a maddening bureaucracy, a poorly developed legal system, summary changes in regulations. But the lure of cheap labor was a powerful draw, more powerful every day as investment havens like Taiwan, Thailand, and South Korea, which used to be low-tech and labor-intensive, ideal for the manufacture of sports shoes, men's pants, and artificial flowers, began going high-end into integrated circuits, TVs, and laptop computers. The clever, industrious Vietnamese, victorious in war and humbled in peace by their years of isolation, would take their place at the low end, grateful for the work. Yes, American investment was going to happen, not as restitution for what we did to them during the war but because American business needed new investment opportunities and Vietnam needed investment capital and jobs. It was only a matter of time, the electricity was in the air. Direct phone links were already in place between Hanoi and the States. The French were putting in a citywide digital touch-tone system. Even now you could dial direct, if you had somebody to call. For the present Hanoi had twenty-five thousand telephones for the entire city of three million people.

I wondered where those American businessmen, used to their expense-account comforts, were going to stay once they got into town. The government had been hoarding a small number of colonial villas. The Metropole had ninety rooms;

the new wing wouldn't be ready until next year. The cavernous Thang Loi, built by the Cubans over on West Lake, was usually filled with tour groups.

Mr. Kha took me on the rounds of the current possibilities: the brand-new Saigon, open just one week, the Sun, the Hoa Binh. Timid young lady receptionists walked me up flights of stairs and down corridors to witness the marvel of individual hot water heaters, flush toilets, grey polyester coverlets on twin beds. The Saigon, the Sun, and the Hoa Binh were Hanoi's best foot forward without foreign assistance. Okay, so the imported plumbing was rinkydink. I tried to envision the faceless local bureaucrat who'd ordered the grey polyester for the beds.

Vietnam is not exactly a country without a developed sense of fabric, design, and color. The ethnic minority groups are famous for their vividly woven cloth; contemporary artists are desperate for work. Evidently it had not occurred to the state to call upon its people to contribute their artistic skills to anything as practical as a hotel room. Of course not. Grey is the only safe color to a bureaucrat's mind.

I perked up briefly as we approached the grand curved driveway of Ministry of Defense Guest House "A," a sprawling colonial mansion where Henry Kissinger had stayed in 1973, when the peace talks got serious. Catherine Deneuve had rested her magnificent head in that same three-room suite during the making of *Indochine*. All Ministry of Defense Guest House "A" needed to make it a top-notch hostelry was a large infusion of money and a team of interior designers with taste. One day it would happen. For now I walked down bare wood corridors, peeking into rooms that were outfitted with army cots and regulation blankets, until the musty odors drove me away.

*   *   *

"Do not, repeat, *do not* miss the Water Puppets," a friend had advised. Luckily for us they were in town for their seasonal engagement, playing three nights a week at their theater at 32 Truong Chinh, out near Lenin Park.

Getting there meant a forty-five-minute drive by cyclo. After a quick consultation, Maggie and I hired two conveyances from the hotel's fleet. They looked like surreys with the fringe on top. Our drivers wore white jackets with the green Pullman logo. So what the hell, we'd roll through the streets like silly rich tourists. I was tired of sneaking around the corner to negotiate a cheaper fare.

Any cyclo ride in Hanoi is apt to be an adventure as the driver pedals through traffic, dodging pedestrians, bicycles, scooters, other cyclos, the occasional car. Illuminated intermittently by the harsh glare of fluorescent wands that serve as street lights, a ride by night is a fast-moving stereopticon of urban impressions: an open-air barbershop where a dapper male client is getting a blow-dry; a night-soil collector announcing his presence by banging his metal cart; Asian music videos delighting their youthful clientele at a dim bar; the sawing, hammering, cement pouring and bricklaying that never cease as the city revs up for its market-economy future; a cascade of twinkling Christmas tree lights festooning hotels and popular eateries, Hanoi's response to the calumny that it is dour and grim.

The small theater was rapidly filling with tour groups when we arrived to claim a front-row bench facing a pool of water and a makeshift curtain.

"What nationality?"

"American!"

The answer got us a program in French. Behind us, some Japanese men got English programs. The international audience—French, Belgians, Austrians, Germans, Japanese,

Dutch—buzzed with anticipation. There wasn't a Vietnamese in sight.

Water Puppets are an original Vietnamese entertainment dating from the twelfth century, at the latest, when news that the king had viewed a performance at a local pagoda was inscribed on a royal stele. For purposes of comparison I'd say that they're sort of like a village Punch and Judy show, Japanese *bunraku*, the shadow puppets of Java, and Billy Rose's Aquacade all rolled into one. About a dozen state-supported companies tour the provinces during various pagoda festivals, where the marionettes and their unseen handlers, maneuvering long poles and invisible strings, still bring down the house.

Sailing into view, the doll-size wood puppets skim the water's surface, planting and harvesting rice, catching fish, chasing ducks and each other in frantic confusion. Fire-breathing dragons! The Dance of the Lions! Magnificent sea battles amid popping firecrackers, billowing smoke, and churning waves! In the surest crowd pleasers, the high and mighty get their comeuppance, or the peasant succumbs to the sorry mishaps and ironic surprises of everyday life. Drums, timbals, and rattles accompany an operatic narration, but words aren't necessary to recognize the universality of the overly confident fisherman and the prize that eludes his net, the arrogant sailors attempting to spear some playful whales that end up capsizing their boat. The Water Puppets are pure buffoon vaudeville that is unselfconsciously philosophic about the powerful forces of nature and war, a perfectly harmonious art form for a uniquely riparian warrior nation.

We laughed and we roared. When a dozen sturdy men and women revealed themselves at the end of the show, our audience of international sophisticates got to its feet and cheered. For ninety minutes we'd each had a chance to be a child again, to revel in illusion and wizardry in, of all places, Vietnam.

But of course in Vietnam! There are a lot of puppet troupes in the country; only some of them perform on water. During the war, Communist rhetoric had invariably, to the point of stupefaction, called the South Vietnamese "the American puppets," "the Saigon puppets," "the puppet army." Even today that's what they're called on monuments describing their annihilation. After seeing the Water Puppets, I understood in one of those eureka flashes that at least at the beginning of their political usage, these phrases must have evoked a powerful image.

"You like the puppets?" the cyclo driver asks on the ride back.

"Oh yes. And you?"

"I like video," he replies.

"Look at that waste," Mr. Kha had groused one morning as we drove over the new bridge. "The lights are still on from last evening. Nobody cares."

"Christmas tree lights, just what Hanoi needs. They're copying Saigon," Barbara Cohen had grumbled on our first night in town when she'd taken us to the disco.

Sitting one afternoon with Eduoard George, the front manager of the Metropole, I'd witnessed a momentary brownout. He leaped from his chair. "No problem. We have our own generator," he sighed with relief seconds later.

I picked up that there was a lot of local concern about electricity.

The month before, the minister of energy had been removed from his post amid charges of corruption. In theory the North has a superabundance of hydroelectric power. The South has an energy shortfall that reaches critical proportions during the dry season, when brownouts occur in Saigon three or four days a week. At issue was an overland power line designed to transfer five hundred kilovolts of electricity from Hoa Binh—a massive hydroelectric station built by the Russians on the Da River below Hanoi—to the energy-deficient South by way of the former Ho Chi Minh Trail. Most of the pole foundations for the overland trunk line were already in place, but the construction had been plagued by faked invoices, theft of materials, delays, cost overruns, and inadequate planning. Naysayers in the National Assembly were already complaining that the entire project was a wasteful, ill-conceived boondoggle. According to their projections, industrial development could exhaust the North's energy surplus by 1995, only one year after the power line's scheduled completion.

I learned this from reading the *Far Eastern Economic Review* while blow-drying my hair in my hotel room.

Patrick was a French filmmaker, in town to gather research for a documentary on the Vietnamese diaspora. Enlivened by his company at Restaurant 202 Hue, where we'd returned for lunch and a second bout with the garlic-sautéed crabs, we invited him to join us later for dinner. Patrick was traveling on a small grant and a lot of schemes. With Gallic charm he declared that he was going to pay back our hospitality by taking me to a little shop on Hang Dao where a woman he knew sold antique watches—Rolexes, Patek Philippes, and other treasures. He pulled up his shirt sleeves to show me the four he'd already purchased.

"Listen, dear friend. The two of us, we are internationalists, no? I collect antique watches. They are my passion. Buy from this woman and sell when you return to New York. You will make back the full cost of your trip!"

"I don't know anything about antique watches, Patrick."

"Ah, this woman, I trust her. She will show you the serial numbers outside and inside the case. The serial numbers will match."

At the shop I put on my glasses to look at the serial numbers. They matched. I examined the watch dials, the oscillating suns and moons, the worn leather straps.

"Patrick, I'm out of my depth here. I'm not buying a watch."

Was it my imagination, or did the watch seller give me a sisterly smile? Probably it was my imagination. She started trading with Patrick.

"One hundred dollar."

"*Impossible*. I give you one hundred for two."

"Two hundred dollar."

"*Non*. One hundred fifty."

Patrick acquired four more watches for the grand total of two hundred dollars. The entire process had happened too rapidly for my sense of ease. I put a big question mark in my notebook next to the address of the little shop on Hang Dao.

Besides Bat Trang pottery and suspect watches, there was just enough, but not too much, for a tourist to buy in Hanoi. Old silver compacts, at twenty to thirty dollars, that were probably intended to hold betel nut or lime paste. Colorful "Ha-Noi" t-shirts hand-embroidered with street scenes of bicycles and cyclos, trees and pagodas. Four-ounce tins of Russian malossol caviar, reminders of a disappearing era, for twelve dollars.

At Tan My, which billed itself as "the famous, well-known embroidery shop" at 109 Hang Gai, Maggie and I picked up some jewel-toned silk shirts, at four to six dollars, that had been cut from stylish Western designs.

I bought a couple of secondhand books as keepsakes. One was *Customs and Culture of Vietnam* by Ann Caddell Crawford, circa 1965, a compilation of wisdom acquired in Saigon by a U.S. Army major's wife: "The most important group in Vietnam, in my opinion, is the plain ordinary people, often heard called 'peasants.' I wish we had a nicer term to denote these fine, long-suffering people. They are very curious about life outside their own areas and are generally friendly."

Dear Ann Caddell Crawford, Your book was on sale for the outrageous sum of ten dollars at the Temple of Literature, which ought to please you even though you're not getting royalties on this pirated facsimile edition printed in Hanoi with pages stuck in the middle that you didn't write. With the trade embargo and all that, you can't blame Hanoi for not honoring the International Copyright Convention, can you?

P.S. You might be interested to know that the giant American bestsellers in Vietnam today, also without regard to copyright laws, are Margaret Mitchell and Danielle Steele.

My second book purchase was *People's War, People's Army* by General Giap, which I found, appropriately enough, at the Army Museum.

Housed in a compound of old French army barracks on a street called Dien Bien Phu, the Army Museum—featuring a huge diorama of that famous victory, and the trophy remains of a downed B-52 in its courtyard—is not a sentimental favorite with most French and American tourists. Aside from some Hanoi schoolchildren, Maggie and I had the place to ourselves. Or so we thought until the photographer, prowling the museum's second-floor veranda for a good overview shot, peeked into a louver-shuttered office and found it humming with U.S. Defense Department types.

The Americans in the Army Museum did not wish to pose for Maggie's camera. They were on an MIA mission, a seemingly endless MIA mission, the details of which I had succeeded in avoiding for years, as I'd avoided most news stories having to do with Vietnam. I am not ashamed to make this confession, because I believe that most people ceased to follow the MIA story somewhere along the line, or knew only in the most general terms that its satisfactory resolution (satisfactory, that is, to the United States) had become the key to opening trade relations with a country where hostilities supposedly ended twenty years ago.

Activity had picked up this particular week in Hanoi after a U.S. researcher working in the Army Museum's archives was handed a cache of GI helmets and boots, and a shopping bag of photo albums. Senator John Kerry, the Vietnam vet and former antiwar activist who is chairman of the Senate Select Committee on POW/MIA Affairs, had arrived in town to push the investigation along to that point on the horizon where everyone—well, no, I think it will never be everyone—could say *finis*.

At what moment in its sad, anguished, convoluted, divisive history should I leap into a capsule discussion of the POW/MIA issue, and how should it be cast? I opt here for the past tense, in the hope that by the time these words appear in print, there will be a resolution, and an end to the trade embargo.

As good a moment as any might be the week after the formal signing of the 1973 Paris peace agreement, when a secret letter from President Richard Nixon dated February 1 assured North Vietnam's prime minister, Pham Van Dong, that the United States was prepared to give $3.25 billion in postwar reconstruction aid. (Promises, promises. Three months earlier, Nixon and Henry Kissinger assured South Vietnam's president, Nguyen Van Thieu, also by secret letter, that the United States was prepared to intervene again if North Vietnam broke the cease-fire agreement.) On February 12, the first American POWs were released in Hanoi. By the end of March, nearly six hundred POWs had been freed. The joy that attended Operation Homecoming could hardly be shared by the families of those men who'd been classified as missing in action, for during the long war they had clung to the hope that their MIA might be alive and a prisoner somewhere.

Treaties, said Charles de Gaulle, preserve their bloom as long as young girls and roses. Instead of dismantling our military bases as stipulated by the Paris agreement, we turned them over to South Vietnam. Within two years the Southern republic was finished, as it would have been a decade or two earlier had we not entered the war in the first place. There was no American gesture of reconciliation toward a unified Vietnam. Instead, relations worsened again during the Carter administration. China and Vietnam, no longer war buddies, were at loggerheads over Pol Pot, especially after Vietnam invaded Cambodia to stop the Khmer Rouge killing fields. Supporting Pol Pot, China invaded Vietnam from the north. Playing the China card, the United States condemned the new Vietnamese "aggression" in Cambodia and—most shockingly—stood behind the genocidal Pol Pot regime in the United Nations, a tricky bit of international maneuvering orchestrated by Zbigniew Brzezinski with the triple aim of opening up China's big untapped market, showing the Soviet Union a thing or two, and continuing to punish Vietnam.

This is where the MIAs fitted in. (My understanding of the MIA question owes nearly everything to H. Bruce Franklin's M.I.A., or Mythmaking in America.) Accountability for the fate of more than two thousand men listed as missing in action became the emotional argument put forward by our government for not normalizing relations with Vietnam, continuing the trade embargo, not anteing up aid for postwar reconstruction, and blocking Vietnam's chances for development loans through the IMF and the World Bank.

One of the tragedies of war is that the bodies of some of the dead are never recovered and some mangled remains cannot be identified, to the perpetual sorrow of family members who must find their solace at the Tomb of the Unknown Soldier. Approximately seventy-nine thousand Americans are still unaccounted for from World War II. More than eight thousand are unaccounted for from the Korean War. At the close of our war in Vietnam, nearly half of the more than two thousand American "missing" were *known* to have died in action—most were airmen whose planes exploded at supersonic speeds—but there had been no way to recover even a microscopic fragment of their mortal remains. As the years went by and our relations with Vietnam did not improve, the "body not recovered" category, which should have become a subdivision of "killed in action," got lumped into the "missing in action" category in official government pronouncements. The combined figure then acquired another dimension, one that was hauntingly strange and conspiratorial, as the unshakable belief of grieving families that a missing son, husband, or father might be a living captive took hold in the popular imagination.

Late in the war, thousands of people who hadn't lost a relative in Vietnam began wearing MIA bracelets as a statement that these men of uncertain fate were not forgotten. After the POWs came home, the MIA bracelet campaign was not discontinued. If proof was needed that evil foreigners kept innocent Americans in makeshift prisons, one could always point to the Beirut hostage crisis, or to the journalists, businessmen, and teachers who were captured at intervals by obscure Shiite sects and languished for years while our government flubbed its diplomacy and bungled rescue missions. Belief that an evil Vietnam still held American prisoners of war, and that callous Washington bureaucrats had written them off, appealed to those on the right who were prone to conspiracy theories and susceptible to outright hoaxes. Intriguing faked photographs surfaced from time to time: shots of a curious configuration in a paddy, supposedly taken on a secret aerial reconnaissance mission, that could be read, if one desired, as a pitiful SOS; a thicket of tropical foliage obscuring gaunt, peering faces that some poor bereft relatives would claim to recognize as missing kin.

By the mid-1980s the myth of the POW alive and starving somewhere in Indochina had moved from the domain of grieving MIA families and their supporters among the lunatic fringe into the mainstream via the Hollywood action movie and stars like Gene Hackman, Chuck Norris, and Sylvester Stallone. Slam-bang entertainments chockablock with awesome computerized special effects, *Uncommon Valor*, *Missing in Action*, and *Rambo* introduced a clutch of sad-eyed hunks with faint, weary smiles and sixties-style headbands who single-handedly reclaimed America's honor. Perhaps intended as nothing more than revenge fantasies, these epic flicks rode a crest of renewed national patriotism. More ominously, they gave credence to and popularized the bizarre delusion not only that live POWs had been abandoned in Vietnam but that cynics in Washington were letting them rot there.

Rambo's evolution was particularly instructive. In *First Blood*, Stallone's initial outing with the John Rambo character, he played a misunderstood Vietnam vet who was suffering from full-blown Post-Traumatic Stress Syndrome and whose buddy had died from Agent Orange. *That* John Rambo, at war with the state of Oregon, was an appealing loser with a heartrending caveman simplicity. For *Rambo:*

First Blood Part II, the silent hero returned to Vietnam to refight the war and rescue a cageful of POWs after delivering his famous line, "Do we get to win this time?" Sylvester Stallone, the man himself, turned out to be a fervent believer in the POW myth and had his halo of authority enhanced by none other than President Ronald Reagan. Star of his own Korean War POW movie in an earlier incarnation, Reagan tripled the Defense Department staff for Vietnam POW/MIA investigations during his term in office.

With Reagan in the White House, the existence of live POWs became an article of faith and an official government position. The presidents who succeeded him found it difficult to reverse the flow, even after American business interests began saying, "Enough, already." Popular myths, including those that have outlived their political usefulness, are hard to shut off.

What it came down to, in late 1993, was a permanent Defense Department POW/MIA office in Hanoi deploying seventy people in the field to investigate known crash sites, not only in Vietnam but in Cambodia and Laos. None of the "live sightings" so dear to the conspiracy theorists panned out, of course, but seventy "discrepancy cases" involving ninety-two men were still being actively pursued. The issue was body remains, not living prisoners.

During the war General William Westmoreland had remarked, echoing others, that the Vietnamese just didn't value human life the way Westerners did. The insistence on dotting the *i* and crossing the *t* on every American MIA twenty years after a catastrophic intervention in which two million Vietnamese died and three hundred thousand remain missing in action seemed like a slow-motion replay of that earlier slur.

On the positive side, the MIA search was putting ten million dollars a year into the Vietnamese economy. American Defense Department teams, operating this time around as lawful visitors to the socialist republic, were paying top dollar for office space, lodging, meals, transportation to remote areas, interpreters, and field guides. In return for Vietnamese cooperation that met their exacting demands, they had agreed to underwrite some flood-control projects.

I didn't want to leave Hanoi. I had caught it at a perfect moment, as it was awakening to change, determinedly optimistic, thrilled to see a friendly American face. The dispirited loss of political innocence apparent in some quarters was more than made up for by an overall and unquenchable national pride, evident in the parks and streets and market arcades, an indomitable belief that to be a citizen in the capital city of the independent Socialist Republic of Vietnam was to be at the center of the universe. Naïve, yes, but a tiny nation that had fought off the military might of two big Western powers was entitled to a grand, if mistaken, belief in its infallible powers, as long as it didn't become a terminal condition. There was no way I could say, like Lincoln Steffens, that I had seen the future and it worked, for the future as originally anticipated by Hanoi's leaders hadn't worked. A tougher revolution lay ahead.

DANANG

Danang was arrivals and departures, B-52s, troop transports, incoming rockets, outgoing refugees. I wanted to skip Vietnam's ugly, depressing central port city, but direct flights to Hue were running only two days a week. So Danang it was, for one morning, and *outathere*. If only the marines had extricated themselves as swiftly.

Danang, March 8, 1965. U.S. Marines wade ashore seven months after the Gulf of Tonkin Resolution. The amphibious landing was a bit of a stunt, a rerun of *The Sands of Iwo Jima* for the older generation, a recruiting-poster image for the kids who were going to fight in the war. Brigadier General Karch flew in by helicopter for the photo op on the beach—a nice little ceremony, short and to the point. Speech by the local mayor, bunch of schoolgirls carrying flowers. Children waved from the side of the road as the truck convoys followed the heavily secured route to the airbase, where South Vietnamese ARVNs, prompted by their American advisers, had strung welcoming banners. The ground phase of the American war in Vietnam had begun.

Back home, students at the University of Michigan called for a one-day moratorium, then conducted an all-night teach-in on March 24. Following Ann Arbor, that year there were teach-ins at Wisconsin, Columbia, NYU, Oregon, Rutgers, Cornell, and Berkeley. A sweet, naive exhilaration marked those early campus protests. Who wasn't naive in those days? Hey, I thought, the students are going to turn this thing around! Instead, the curse of the war brought on the worst generational conflict in American history. "Don't trust anyone over thirty."

Bracket the Danang landing and the college teach-ins as one set of related events. Mark another set of brackets ten years down the line.

Danang, March 27, 1975. Two Boeing 727s chartered in Saigon land at the airbase to begin evacuating panicked refugees. A thousand frantic ARVNs and their families trample the security fences when the first plane touches down. Soldiers mobbing the tarmac fire on the crowd as they punch and kick their way aboard. Someone hurls a hand grenade. The only civilians who make it onto the flight are two women and a baby thrown into the cabin by a desperate mother left stranded on the field. As the plane lifts off, stowaways clutching the retracting wheels lose their grasp. Cameras on the second Boeing film them falling into the South China Sea.

Arrivals and departures were the story of Danang. In the second century A.D. the region belonged to the decentralized kingdom of Champa, a Hinduized, seafaring Malayo-Polynesian people of remarkable artistic talent who dotted the landscape with ornate sandstone towers when they weren't raiding their neighbors, the Viets and the Khmers. By the fifteenth century the Chams had been squeezed southward into near extinction as the Viets moved down the peninsula in an inexorable migration that was not unlike the big push westward in the United States. (Today the descendants of the old Chams, many of whom embrace a local version of Islam, are one of Vietnam's nearly sixty minority groups.)

In the 1850s a French armada engaged the forces of the Vietnamese emperor Tu Duc at the site of the present-day harbor, leaving a garrison that fell to malaria and cholera within a year. Ceded to France a decade later, the town, which the Europeans called Tourane, became the main port for Vietnam's skinny central region—the protectorate the French called Annam, to distinguish it from the north, called Tonkin, and the colony in the south called Cochin China.

Danang was occupied by the Japanese during World War II and became a Viet Minh stronghold, taking up arms in 1945 against the returning French forces. A decade later the Geneva agreements placed the rebel city under the South's control. Regrouping under Communist leaders, the Viet Minh melted into the countryside to continue their guerrilla campaign. We called them Viet Cong.

Danang's next incarnation came after the marines landed to beef up "Eye" Corps (I Corps), the South's faltering command for its five northernmost provinces. It became a boom town, the region's nerve center for an anguished decade, home to the key airbase, harbor, troop-transport facility, and resupply zone for the north of the South. The population bloated from fifty thousand under the French to more than six hundred thousand as refugees streamed in from the provinces, uprooted from their land by artillery fire, search-and-destroy operations, and bombardments sometimes preceded by air-dropped leaflets:

The U.S. Forces have joined with the forces of South Vietnam to rid your village of Viet Cong agents and protect your lives. The Viet Cong hide among innocent women and children in your villages to fire upon troops and aircraft. If the Viet Cong in this area use you or your village for this purpose, you can expect death from the sky.

Do not let your lives and your homes be destroyed. Do not let the Viet Cong be the reason for the death of your loved ones.

Report all Viet Cong locations immediately. Once the Viet Cong are eliminated, peace will come to South Vietnam. Help the Government of South Vietnam help you!

By the end of 1966 Danang airport was the third busiest in the world, right behind Chicago/O'Hare and Saigon. It had the longest, noisiest jet runway of them all, a 10,000-foot strip with high-speed turnoffs and sections for taxiing and parking the C-130 transports that brought in fresh troops and shipped them out, haggard and demoralized, twelve months later, thirteen months if they were marines. B-52s, Phantoms, Skyhawks, and Raiders roared in and out on tactical missions. A huge concrete apron accommodated helicopter pads, steel-spined "Wonder Arch" hangars, a 160,000-barrel fuel depot, repair shops, and truck garages, plus PX stores, mess halls, and barracks.

The ARVN air force was allotted a slice of the field. The rest of the base was an American city, with its own generators and water purification plants, three hospitals, four movie theaters, bowling alleys, tennis courts, a radio station, cafeterias dispensing soda, hot dogs, and ice cream, and separate bars for officers and enlisted men. Triage units at the naval support hospital tended the wounded who were med-evacked in by choppers; cases with a chance of survival were evacuated back to the States. Nearby, a restaurant with shatterproof Lucite chandeliers employed Filipino waiters to serve New York–cut steaks.

A shantytown called Dogpatch sprang up in the muddy flats on the base's barbed-wire perimeter, catering to needs and desires that couldn't be satisfied inside the cocoon. Here the Vietnamese squeezed into hovels of cardboard, packing crate, and corrugated tin, with no running water or sewerage system. Some were permitted on base to do laundry, cleaning, and menial labor. Others scavenged, pilfered, peddled drugs, pimped, or prostituted themselves to eke out a living.

The first year of marine operations, a village called Cam Ne burned on our TV screens. Informed that a cluster of hamlets a few miles from the airbase was harboring VC, the marines invited Morley Safer of CBS to film them in action. What Safer and his cameraman found and filmed was the torching without provocation of 150 thatched huts.

I was among the millions of viewers who watched Cam Ne burn on the evening news, ignited by flamethrowers and Zippo lighters. Another agitated viewer was the president of the United States, who blasted CBS chief Frank Stanton with his full range of expletives the next morning. The gist of LBJ's diatribe was that Safer had to be a dirty Communist.

Nobody ever claimed that there was a shortage of VC, or of general unrest, in the vicinity. The infantry sustained most of its losses on foot patrols that ran into ambushes, sniper fire, booby traps, and mines as they proceeded warily through fields and hamlets. Periodic mortar attacks on the airfield gave rise to its nickname, Rocket City. The Buddhist "struggle move-ment" of 1966 drew local ARVNs, civil servants, and dock workers to its cause until General Ky himself came up from Saigon with loyalist troops to crush the rebels. A VC mortar and rocket attack the following year destroyed seventy-five million dollars' worth of aircraft on the field. By 1968 the entire First Marine Division was deployed in the city's defense during the coordinated attacks of the Tet Offensive.

In the spring of 1975, after the United States Congress cut military support to a trickle, the most heavily defended city in South Vietnam collapsed with a squeak and a squeal as North Vietnamese army units motored in, meeting little resistance. Proficient at war, unknowing of peace, they inherited a collapsed economy and a populace in an acute state of turmoil and fear. In a matter of months, former ARVN officers and civilians who'd been tainted by their American connections were arrested and sent to labor camps for "reeducation." Some of the "politically undesirable" returned after two years, others spent ten years in detention. Citified refugees were resettled in new agricultural zones on the cratered, napalmed land in the outlying districts. Exploding shells, bombs, and mines claimed three thousand casualties in the first three years of peace.

The war-weary city methodically erased nearly every vestige of the American presence, changing street signs, finding new uses for buildings, shipping scrap metal from the behemoth airbase to buyers in Japan. The abandoned U.S. consulate was turned into a war crimes museum, the empty press center became a fish-processing plant. New foreign ships arrived at the harbor carrying Russian technicians and advisers who expounded their unworkable theories of centralized planning. A pared-down Danang of textile mills and canneries developed a modest shipping trade with the Eastern bloc nations until their demise. Danang is still the largest port of central Vietnam, but it is not what you'd call a tourist attraction.

Maggie and I took a fifty-minute early morning flight from Hanoi, landing uneventfully on the empty tarmac. Rumor had it that Air Vietnam's monopoly over in-country travel was about to be broken by Air France, but meanwhile, passengers hoped for the best on the government airline's aging secondhand fleet. Our small Russian Tupelov had been outfitted for the defunct German Democratic Republic. I didn't need to ask; the cabin signs were flashing "*Nicht Rauchen.*"

Mr. Kha was continuing with us on this leg of the trip. He

poked around the terminal, looking for the guide from Danang Tourism while we collected our bags.

We were wondering if there'd been a foul-up when we were approached by a scowling young man wearing a rakish neck scarf. "I was *howlding* a sign," he enunciated loudly.

"Oh, I'm sorry."

"Now we *gaow* to the *awf*ice to get permissions."

Meekly we followed him to a waiting Peugeot. "Did you understand what he was saying?" I whispered to Maggie.

"He seems to have a chip on his shoulder," she whispered back.

Tran Tra—I made a note that "Tra" was pronounced "Cha"—never loosened up during the time he was with us, or rather while *we* were with *him*. With broad high cheekbones and equine teeth, he knew that he was good-looking in a sullen, dangerous way. In any other country I'd have left my musings at that, but because this was Vietnam, I made the connection to a classic face from the television screens. Tra was too young to have fought in the war, but he had the determined bearing of a Viet Cong fighter.

Tra had peacetime problems: a wife and baby in Danang and a girlfriend in Hue. The system had plucked him from his working-class roots, rewarded him with what passed for English lessons, and promoted him to a job he didn't like, though it was considered a plum. Tra soldiered through it like a martinet. I found myself working overtime to crack his facade of the injured party. Early in our time together, Maggie quit trying. When we said goodbye to him six days later, it was with a sigh of relief on both sides. Now, when I reflect upon Tra, my feelings are warmer. He was suffering from a welter of mental contradictions in a country where the rules were changing on him so rapidly that it was hard for him to know how to behave.

Cung, our driver, was a sweetie who took it upon himself to jolly Tra out of his bad humor in a steady stream of melodic Vietnamese. Cung spoke no English, but he did more than his share to keep the five of us on an even keel when we were crowded into his area of responsibility on the road.

While Tra was running our passports and permissions through the tourist office, we crossed the road to the harbor side and wandered into the government gift shop. The dusty display cases were uninviting, filled with mass-produced "handicrafts" that had lost the inspiration of their original designs. A bored sales staff couldn't have cared less whether or not we bought the lacquer box or the statuette of the boy on the water buffalo. I can't say I blamed them. Every creative impulse that goes stale in a Communist country is represented in its government gift shop. Taste and variety are the first things to disappear.

Papers in order, we headed for the Cham museum. The Ecole Française d'Extrême-Orient built a fine colonial mansion in 1915 to house a representative selection of sandstone friezes and sculptures that private collectors had unearthed— that is, chiseled and sawed from their niches—at the abandoned ruins of the departed Chams. Plenty of other Cham treasures were crated and shipped to Paris, but the museum was still the best place in the world to see what beauty the Chams had wrought.

Cham art is monumental in size, exquisite in detail, an eclectic mix of Hindu deities and legends that gradually incorporated Buddhist themes as the Cham people underwent a religious conversion. At the museum, the earliest sculptures date from the seventh century, and three connecting galleries around a courtyard follow the Cham civilization over a time frame of seven hundred years. Unshuttered windows bathe the sandstone statues and friezes in natural light.

Not enough light for Maggie, however. The photographer planted her tripod in the courtyard and went to work. I took my time in the galleries, strolling past awesome sea monsters, mythical lions, smiling elephants, prancing apsaras, proud Sivas, and a lot of lingams—huge phalluses of stone.

Cambodia's temples of Angkor, which I'd been privileged to visit the year before, gave me a basic framework for what I was seeing. I wasn't knowledgeable enough to distinguish Cham art from Khmer art (Bernard Philippe Groslier, director of the Angkor Conservancy before the war forced his departure in 1972, admitted that even he sometimes got confused), but I could appreciate certain related features. The Chams didn't build vast, citylike temple complexes with the epic symmetries of Angkor Wat, or indulge in the moody surrealism of the Bayon, the haunting heart of Angkor Thom. Their towers and sanctuaries were smaller affairs, but like their Khmer neighbors, whose cities they frequently sacked, they invested cosmic significance in phallic representations. Apsaras, the dancing, bare-breasted maidens, were the ubiquitous representation, in both cultures, of female beauty.

A coy young elephant god resting on a pedestal in the first gallery—Ganesha, son of Siva—was the statue I fell in love with and wanted to take home. This Ganesha was a baby elephant, too young to have tusks. I patted its stone trunk. The perfectly preserved piece carved by an unknown Cham artist in the seventh century had been found at My Son, seventy miles south of Danang, the most important of the historic Cham sites.

My Son's red-brick Cham towers were a Viet Cong sanctuary during the war; the surrounding hills provided a good haven. Our marines took to calling the valley Dodge City for the sniper fire they encountered on patrols, and declared My

Son a free-fire zone, which meant that B-52s could drop their ordnance on the ancient site anytime they were in the vicinity. French archeologists lodged a protest with Washington after the finest Cham towers were reduced to rubble.

Archeology got its start in Vietnam when the French opened the Ecole Française d'Extrême-Orient in 1898, choosing Hanoi as a base of operations for exploratory digs throughout Indochina. From brash, clumsy beginnings the young science matured, as it did elsewhere, gradually abandoning the romantic quest for temples and treasures of "lost" civilizations in favor of the less glamorous, quantified search, deeper down in the ground, for the fossil remains of Stone Age cultures.

Among the dreams that the canny revolutionist Ho Chi Minh nurtured during his years in exile, archeology came to occupy a prominent place. It's possible that the great museums of London and Paris, brimming with the cultural artifacts of less fortunate nations, served as his inspiration. (We know that Ho was an inveterate museumgoer.) In any event, Ho seized on the idea that archeological science could provide hard evidence of Vietnam's national identity and unique heritage independent of Chinese or French domination. Just months after announcing the birth of the new republic in 1945, he signed Decree 65, creating the Institute of Archeology at the University of Hanoi. During the ensuing wars for independence, pioneering excavations were carried out in the north by Russians, Bulgarians, and East Germans working with their Vietnamese counterparts. Little news of their work ever reached the West.

A Russian archeologist, P. I. Boriskovskii, produced a major study proposing that Vietnam's Stone Age differed from Europe's Stone Age in the extensive use of bamboo and shells, instead of flint, for tools. Boriskovskii's theory makes perfect sense if you think about it. Use what you've got. In A.D. 938 a Vietnamese military genius, Ngo Quyen, drove a thicket of bamboo stakes into the Bach Dang River to trap an invading Chinese fleet at low tide. A bamboo punji stake, sharpened to a point, hardened over flame, and camouflaged on a trail, could penetrate the sole of a GI's combat boot and impale him to the spot. Bamboo remains central to the fabric of Vietnamese life and survival in the countryside, used for everything from building materials for houses to the cunning little baskets that carry pigs to market.

Trivia Test for Americans

Question: What American general came out of retirement to warn that unless North Vietnam stopped its aggression, "we're going to bomb them back into the Stone Age."

Answer: Curtis LeMay.

"We are crossing the Han River on the American bridge." Tra swivels his head toward the back seat as he chants in his peculiar singsong.

"Really!"

"We are passing the American base."

Maggie adjusts the lens on her camera.

"No photographs."

"Why not?"

"It is not permitted."

We stare at the rows of Quonsets. What could make a barbed-wire enclosure of corrugated metal hangars verboten to cameras? So they're using our old Quonsets to house our old Chinooks and Hueys. Big deal.

"And now we are taking the American road to Hoi An."

"Really!"

My little cries of "Really!" are the best I can muster. Curious sightseeing, to say the least. Nice little steel-reinforced concrete bridge, very smooth surface on that macadam road.

I feel a surge of American pride. Good job, Brown and Root, good job, Seabees, you built 'em to last and they're lasting.

"Well, it's really terrific that you're finding the road and the bridge so useful."

Tra swivels and stares. "Yes, very useful."

In fifteen minutes we were in Hoi An, one of Vietnam's best-kept secrets, though not, I suspect, for long.

As far back as the sixteenth century, Hoi An was a bustling port of call for merchant ships that sailed from India and Persia to pick up Vietnamese silk and ceramics, beeswax, spices, ivory, fragrant sandalwood, and mother-of-pearl. Portuguese traders knew it as Fai Fo, a place of skulduggery and nefarious intrigues, when they sailed from Macao to open a post in the early 1600s, summoning their missionaries to begin making converts in the seamy harbor. The Dutch East India Company, fresh from its triumphs in Indonesia and Ceylon, muscled its way in briefly. "The Annamites insist on setting their own prices," wrote a horrified seventeenth-century British trader. After the Mings were overthrown by the Manchus in 1644, refugees from China's coastal cities fled to Hoi An, staying to prosper in riverfront shops. Agents for Japanese trading companies built their own separate enclave to welcome their incoming ships. With excellent business acumen, the merchant-traders intermarried with Vietnamese women. The wives knew the territory, striking the best bargains with inland farmers who brought their produce to the lucrative market by barge and packhorse.

For four months starting each spring when the winds were at their most favorable and a hundred Chinese junks and vessels from other nations might anchor offshore, the Hoi An fair was in high gear. Coins of all realms were accepted, warehouses emptied quickly, imports and exports were duly taxed. Topping the list of profitable exports were silk yarn and cloth, sugar, gold, sea-swallow nests (made of high-protein bird saliva, gathered from offshore islands, and still highly prized for their medicinal value), fragrant sandalwood (the fuel of choice for funeral pyres), cinnamon, cardamom, nutmeg, pepper, dried areca nuts (the chief ingredient, along with betel leaves and lime paste, for the mild narcotic pastime of betel cud chewing), ceramics, rosewood, tortoiseshell, ivory, and rhinoceros horn. Desirable imports were leather goods, woolens, felt, silver, bronze kettles, cosmetics, mirrors, and firearms.

Natural ecological changes were to deal the port of Hoi An a fatal blow. By the time French warships sailed toward Vietnam in the 1850s, Hoi An's estuary had become so laden with silt that it was too treacherous for large-vessel navigation. The French planted their flag at the deepwater cove to the north, now Danang.

Eclipsed by the newer and larger port, Hoi An's riverfront shop-houses remained as they were in the early part of the nineteenth century, moldering along with a jumble of Chinese temples and a ceremonial covered bridge reportedly built by the Japanese. The old port did not escape the two Indochina wars, however. An American command post superseded a French command post; South Korean soldiers were bivouacked in the new part of town. The VC mounted an attack in the Tet Offensive. Hoi An's shallow estuary was one of the embarkation points for fleeing ARVNs in 1975.

Restoration projects guided by the Hoi An Tourist Service

and Monuments Management Authority have been under way since 1986, when *doi moi*, the nationwide economic initiative program, suddenly made such things possible. The entire town seems possessed by an entrepreneurial spirit that is perfectly in keeping with its old trading-post habits. With dollar signs in the present inhabitants' eyes, the historic port is now a tourist's mecca en route to becoming a Colonial Williamsburg. I don't mean that unkindly. I adored Hoi An. There's nothing remotely like it anywhere else in Vietnam. Scholars report that there is even a distinct Hoi An dialect, a low drawl that is neither of the North nor of the South.

Not everyone in Vietnam approves of Hoi An's energetic new entrepreneurs. When my baggage was being checked for the second time at Tan Son Nhut airport in Saigon, a customs inspector looked me in the eye and taunted, "Did you buy any antiques in Hoi An?"

I didn't, but I wanted to, and would have if I hadn't thought they'd be confiscated down the line. For five dollars cheerfully aggressive merchants at outdoor stalls were hawking ceramic plates with simple fish designs that they claimed were from old Hoi An. Guessing that they probably were, I virtuously passed them by.

With Tra in the lead, we wandered through several red-and-gold Chinese temples, each one more ornate than the last, all built in the eighteenth century and enlarged in the nineteenth by competing congregations wishing to retain their ties to the provinces of their birth. In an odd juxtaposition on the nearby streets, new cafes with striped awnings added a touch of Marseilles. There was even a small hotel.

"Mr. Kha," I wailed, "why didn't you tell me about the hotel? We could have stayed here."

"Eighteen rooms, four are air-conditioned," he reeled off quickly. "It opened after you made your arrangements."

Tra led us to the Japanese covered bridge as a light rain began falling. Mr. Kha, who'd been uncharacteristically quiet all day, had something he wanted to show me. "Look," he said, pointing to a set of wood doors. "Here is a Chinese temple in the middle of the bridge."

"It is the Japanese temple," Tra tartly corrected.

"It is the Chinese temple."

Suddenly they were scrapping like terriers. Maggie and I had experienced similar eruptions that came out of nowhere. Squalls to release tension, like the sudden downpour.

"Gentlemen, I don't care if it's a Chinese temple or a Japanese temple. It is *raining*."

Like a living tableau of a Hiroshige print, we scurried under the guides' umbrellas toward a restaurant. Cung was already there, waiting for us.

"Ah," I said, happy with anticipation, "I know something about Hoi An that's going to surprise you. Tra, this is where we get the special soup that you can't get anywhere else, right?"

"That is another restaurant."

"*Another* restaurant? Then *why*—" I bit my tongue. Tra withdrew into a pout. Late in the meal I remembered to order a coke for Cung.

After lunch Tra announced he was taking us to the Tan Ky trading house, a two-story riverfront dwelling belonging to a family of Vietnamese merchants from the heyday of Hoi An. We dutifully trooped behind him, assuming we were headed for a little museum. Tra banged on a numbered door. "The old guy in there doesn't hear so well," he laughed, banging harder. We were ready to go elsewhere when the door opened and an apologetic youth ushered us inside.

The old, walleyed owner of the Tan Ky house, a direct descendant of the original owner five generations back, was so frail he could not move from his chair. His wife and the assistant hovered in the background while we arranged ourselves as best we could in their cluttered parlor. The dark, wood-paneled room encrusted with mother-of-pearl was an eccentric treasure trove of curio cabinets, Chinese glass paintings, beribboned sabers, and feathered, stuffed birds suspended on chains from great carved beams that supported the ceiling. In the anteroom a new cement well had been dug into the floor.

The assistant brought tea. We poured and sipped in the ossified silence while the living relic coughed into his hand.

"Ask him whatever you wish," Tra prompted loudly. "The owner speaks English."

Performance, ladies, please.

Less put upon, I suspected, than the ancient gentleman obliged to perform for his "guests," Maggie and I expressed our admiration for his beautiful house. The ceiling beams were carved from the wood of the jackfruit tree, he rasped. The mother-of-pearl insets at the corners were Chinese poems. "The style of the house incorporates many Chinese elements," he wheezed between coughs, "but there are many original Vietnamese elements in the design." It was a canned recitation, a speech for the guides.

His ancestors made their fortune by trading in cinnamon, tea, silk, and areca nuts, he told us. He worshiped his ancestors in this parlor; their framed portraits were on the wall. Probably he would be the last Tan Ky descendant to live in Hoi An. His son, an engineer in Danang, had another life and no interest in this one.

With the old man's permission, I explored the rear part of the house, which opened onto the river. Palm fronds sheltered a covey of rowboats beached on the opposite bank. A boatman paddled by swathed in rain gear, his face obscured by a conical straw hat. Except for a clean blue plastic slop bucket placed near the doorway, the twentieth century had not intruded on the scene.

Returning to the parlor, I noticed a table of knickknacks and a price card. The old lady stirred. I took the hint. The last descendant of the Tan Ky merchant family in Hoi An was supplementing his income by selling cheap figurines. Maggie and I made a small contribution to the upkeep of the house before we departed.

Tired of touring temples, the guides took a break, letting us traipse by ourselves through the Assembly Hall of the Fukien (Fujian) Congregation, a meeting house built in the seventeenth century for one of the wealthier Chinese communities in town. I barreled past an altar, craning my neck at a life-size ceramic horse, and collided head-on with a presentation chart on an easel.

"Hey, Maggie," I called. "Come look at this!" Three different color schemes and coordinated patterns, as sophisticated as Scalamandre, were tacked to the chart.

"Hi, you American? Where ya from?"

The engaging face that went with the chipper American voice belonged to a wiry Vietnamese in a sport shirt, I guessed in his forties.

"You're supposed to choose the pattern you like best and then make a donation to the restoration."

"I think I prefer the middle pattern," I said, shaking his hand. "Who are you, a tour leader who lost his group, or an official representative of Hoi An?"

He winced. "Oh no, they won't let me be a guide. I just help out at the temple."

Puzzled, I told him his English was the best I'd heard in Vietnam.

"Thanks," he replied. "I used to translate for You-said, but I'm a little rusty."

"You translated for *what?*"

"You-said."

His face fell when I shook my head. "I'm sorry, I don't think I understand."

"U-S-A-I-D."

"Oh! You mean USAID!"

"Right!"

Relieved, we shook hands again.

Linh wasn't fooling when he said he didn't have a job. To pass the time he hung out at the temple, chatting up tourists when they asked about the color schemes on the easel, explaining in his uncanny American accent that if they cared to help the Fukien restoration, the man behind the desk would take their money and the old calligrapher sitting at his side would paint their names on red cloth and pin them onto the wall.

The Fukien donors' wall was an international hall of fame at very affordable prices.

Pierre & Lucette	Bob	Anna
France	England	Holland
D5,000	D5,000	D500
Helga & Ulrike	Jean-Claude	Andre
Germany	Belge	France
D10,000	D200	D5,000

Ceremoniously Maggie and I donated ten thousand dong, writing our names on a piece of paper. We watched the calligrapher copy them perfectly with his brush.

Maggie & Susan
USA
D10,000

Linh held the chair while the calligrapher climbed up to pin our square of red cloth to the top of the wall.

"How long do the names stay up there, Linh?"

"They take them down at Tet and start over again."

"Hey, that's in two months. Tell the man in charge to keep ours up longer."

"He says maybe they'll keep yours up longer."

Promises, promises. Maggie and I bade a formal *cam on* and *chao* to the men at the desk. We said a reluctant goodbye to Linh.

"I wish you could be our guide, Linh. We understand your English perfectly."

"Before you leave, could I ask your advice about my future?" he said.

I braced myself for what was coming. "Don't even think about it, Linh. Put the Orderly Departure Program out of your mind. You don't want to come to the States. I read in our newspapers that a lot of Vietnamese aren't doing so well. Some are coming back here."

"That's what I've heard, too." He looked crestfallen nonetheless.

Under the Program for Orderly Departure administered by the United Nations High Commission for Refugees, Vietnamese seeking to reunite with their families abroad, Amerasians, and former U.S. employees could now sign up for legal exit papers instead of risking their lives in boats on the open sea. Boat People who wished to return to Vietnam—an increasingly attractive alternative to the limbo of a Hong

Kong detention center—were guaranteed a stake of four hundred dollars and a promise of no reprisals. More than thirty-two thousand Boat People had already taken the repatriation option. Most of the returnees were doing very well thanks to the UN nest egg, which equaled two years of wages.

"Things are improving here, Linh, aren't they? My best advice is to stay put." I almost said, "Trust me."

"So you think I should wait for the embargo to lift? That was my other thought, to wait for the lifting of the embargo. If American businessmen come to Hoi An, do you think they would want an experienced translator?"

I assured him they'd snap him up the moment he opened his mouth. I meant it.

On the road again, heading for Hue. Hue is over a mountain pass in the opposite direction from Hoi An, so we double back through Danang to begin heading north.

Tra calculates that we have time for a look-see at China Beach, an in-country R & R area during the war. R & R was "rest and recreation," or "rape and run" for the slam, bam, you-number-one aspect of the recreation. China Beach was also the site of the Ninety-fifth Evacuation Hospital featured in the television series that had a short run a few years ago, to good reviews.

I get the feeling from Tra that Danang Tourism has high hopes for China Beach. They seem to think that with the TV recognition factor and the cement-block hotel the Russians put up in 1985, Americans will soon be sunning themselves here in droves. I'm not so sure. I know that Vietnam has miles and miles of beautiful, unspoiled, palm-fringed beaches, and I'm on assignment for a magazine called *Travel & Leisure*, but somehow I can't reconcile a beach blanket and suntan lotion with Vietnam. Not in my lifetime anyway. Leave it for the post–Vietnam War generation.

Plus, I'd caught an episode or two of *China Beach* on the tube. It wasn't as funny as *M*A*S*H*, and it didn't have a great theme song, or Alan Alda.

Plus, I'd read Lewis Puller's account of a day's R & R on China Beach with his platoon, and they weren't sunning themselves or playing volleyball. They were drinking hard and psyching themselves by swapping tales about Puller's legendary father, the most decorated marine in history. Back on patrol a few days later, Chesty Puller's young son stepped on a booby trap, losing both legs at the hip and most of his fingers.

Plus, it's raining. Maybe not rain to a Vietnamese, but rain to an American. A very fine drizzle.

We pull up to a circular concrete pavilion. Tra makes his announcement. "China Beach."

"You buy from me."

"You buy from me."

"You buy from me."

One car with two tourists in it has raised the hopes of fifteen women in fifteen identical knickknack stalls. We must be the only live action they've seen all day.

I descend a few steps to the beach, chased by a pack of urchins hawking peanut candy. On a clear day maybe the emerald waters and distant mountains really do rival Waikiki. I've got grey pounding surf and a scene out of Tennessee Williams' *Suddenly, Last Summer*. (How did she die? Oh, didn't you hear? She was devoured by urchins at China Beach.)

Di di, the GIs used to say. *Scram*. But that was back then, when we turned a generation of kids into little beggars. This can't be the Socialist Republic of Vietnam twenty years later.

"You buy from me."

"You buy from me."

"Hey, ladies, I can't buy from all of you."

At the kiosks the sisterhood was peddling some of the ugliest trinkets I'd ever seen—flying fish ineptly carved out of porous sandstone, your choice of small, medium, or large. The trinkets were so unappealing that it occurred to me that the only conceivable reason for their existence was to shake some dollars from guilty tourists.

I bought two fish with chipped tails for fifteen thousand dong ($1.50). Souvenirs of China Beach.

The Hai Van Pass between Danang and Hue, a famous section of National Highway 1, winds along the mountainous coastline at an altitude of six thousand feet above sea level. The route was known as the Mandarin Road when Hue was the imperial capital of central Vietnam. The French called it the Col des Nuages, Pass of the Clouds. I could see why. During the two and a half hours it took us to drive the scenic pass, it was socked in by its usual fog and rain. I'll take it on faith that we wound by several charming fishing villages, a Nguyen Dynasty wall, the remains of some World War II Japanese pillboxes, and a French fort. Sniper fire from behind the outcrops in weather like this did not endear Hai Van to Americans during our war.

"Down below you may see the *raihl*way."

"The what, Tra?"

He glared as if I were some sort of simpleton. "The RAIHLway."

Obviously communication was going to be hopeless for the next six days. Morosely I stared out the window. "Hey, I see tracks!"

Vindicated, Tra flashed me a triumphant smile.

We continued riding to the steady drum of the rain. "Tra, tell me again so I can get it right in my notebook. What's the name of the Hai Van Pass in English?"

"The Pass of the *Auschen* and the Clouds."

"I'm missing a word in there."

"*Auschen, Auschen*," the guide from Danang shouted.

Silently I appealed to our man from Hanoi.

"*Uh*-shun, *uh*-shun," Mr. Kha urgently repeated.

"I've got it! The Pass of the Ocean and the Clouds!"

She says she's got it. Henry Higgins and Eliza Doolittle on the Hai Van Pass. Wait a second . . .

The raihn in Spaihn stahys maihnly in the plaihn.

"Tra, where did you learn your English?"

"In Danang, of course."

"From whom?"

"From a Vietnamese teacher. Of course."

"Who taught him, Tra? Who taught your teacher?"

"A man from Aus*traihlya*."

Cockney to Aussie to Viet. From that point on I found it easier to comprehend Tra.

The next silence was broken by Mr. Kha. "I myself learned my English in Hanoi. But I was sent to Hungary for polishing."

Mr. Kha took it like a sport when we broke out laughing.

"But to be sent to Hungary was an honor!"

HUE

"Hue," wrote Somerset Maugham in the 1920s, "is built on both sides of a wide river, crossed by a bridge, and its hotel is one of the worst in the world." To which I will add, you pronounce it "Hway," the river is the Huong, called the Perfume in English, and you can change hotels now if you wish, but you can't do anything about the weather. Hue is the rain capital of Vietnam, with yearly downpours of 109 inches. In keeping with tradition, it drizzled on and off during the time we were there.

Hue slipped in and out of our national consciousness during the war. Buddhist uprisings, then the Tet Offensive of 1968. Those were the two Big Stories.

I felt melancholic, uneasy, and slightly defrauded in this old imperial capital in the central plains. For one thing, Hue isn't an "ancient" city, although I'd read that description a hundred times. Not that the locale is short on history. The first known settlement at Hue was an encampment of the Chinese Han army in the second century B.C. Chams prospered in the region in the early centuries A.D. Between the tenth and the sixteenth centuries, warring factions of Viets and Chams struggled to capture and hold the riverine expanse near the South China Sea. In the seventeenth and eighteenth centuries, the site became a royal metropolis called Phu Xuan, a trading port and autonomous capital of the Vietnamese Nguyen warlords who finally vanquished the Chams. However, not a vestige of Phu Xuan's architectural patrimony, or of any prior settlement, survived. The carved teak palaces and lacquered colonnades fell to the ravages of time, weather, and warfare as the Nguyens battled their northern kin, the Trinhs. The Tay Son rebellion, a peasant uprising in the late eighteenth century, also took its toll. The famous imperial citadel of Hue where American and North Vietnamese troops mauled each other in the 1968 offensive was built from scratch in the early part of the nineteenth century. "Ancient" caught on in the States through a mistaken translation of *ancienne capitale*, which really means "former capital city."

With the shining exception of Maugham, foreigners used to get misty-eyed when they spoke of Hue's charms—the serenity of the Perfume River, the tree-shaded promenades, the cultured refinement of Hue's poets and scholars, the pale, slender grace of Hue's beautiful women. It became a cliché among hard-bitten journalists during the war, exposed perhaps to one too many a hard-bitten Saigonese hooker, to exclaim, "Ah, Hue!" before launching into breathless raptures over the swanlike schoolgirls peddling their bicycles in flowing white *ao dais*. Even today, Vietnamese men are quick to say that Hue's women are the most beautiful in Vietnam.

After a couple of days in the city, I could see that the smooth, pale complexions, regular features, and tall, willowy bodies of the women *were* of another order from the traits of the sunburnt Vietnamese peasant or the slash-and-burn highlander bent over the fields. So, of course, were the pale complexions, regular features, and willowy bodies of the men. Hue is a university town whose elite mandarin scholars once led Vietnam in music, literature, medicine, and astronomy. Interestingly enough, Hue's privileged students also led Vietnam in revolution. Its premier academy, Quoc Hoc, now a trade school, produced such alumni as Ho Chi Minh, Pham Van Dong, and Vo Nguyen Giap, the three top stars in Vietnam's Communist pantheon. "Ah, Hue!" Another scholar, first in his class, was Ngo Dinh Diem, the first embarrassing miracle man we installed in the South.

Hue is a symbol more than it is a city. For the international community, it is doomed to remain, at least in my lifetime, a fragile reminder of wartime horror, the Vietnamese equivalent of Dresden. Physically it stands in the center of the country as tangible proof that the two halves of Vietnam are one, but the proof resides in a handful of tombs and bombed palaces that belonged to an abusive feudal monarchy whose existence only accidentally coincided with the national aspirations of its people. A world apart from the scooter-whizzing, money-hungry Saigonese or the stoic, politically correct Northerners of steely Hanoi, its citizens seem ineffably sad. I began to suspect during my time in the city that for Vietnam's socialist republic Hue is a flawed, ambiguous emblem, one that the Hanoi government doesn't know quite what to do with, except to dangle it as a magnet for tourists and foreign aid. Even Hue's status as a center of learning is a trifle iffy; the real academic action today is in Hanoi and Saigon. With little commerce or industry, the twin heartbeats that make a city a city, Hue, I felt, was dead at the core.

Dog-tired from the overland drive from Danang, Maggie and I checked into the government-owned and -operated Perfume River Hotel, a.k.a. the Huong Giang, on the right bank of the river, the old French side. We ate a disappointing cold meal in the empty fourth-floor dining room, which was preparing to close for the evening. Tall, mournful waiters, tricked out in polyester mandarin costumes, served us *banh bao*, a gelatinous steamed rice dumpling that is a specialty of Hue. *Banh bao* is either an acquired taste or not at its best served cold at the Huong Giang Hotel. I suspected the latter; our dumplings had the chewy consistency of rubber.

Our two guides and driver had given us the brush-off, or so it appeared. Spotting them in a huddle at the far end of the long, empty room, we figured they'd had enough of our scintillating company for one day. This may well have been true, but it wasn't the reason they were avoiding us. It's amazing that we were so obtuse. Segregation at mealtimes is customary when guides and tourists check into hotels on the road. We were paying guests; their cheap meals and lodgings were included in our package.

I'd requested, and received, a room with a terrace overlooking the Perfume River—pardon me, the Song Huong. From the little balcony I could see the hotel's tour boat, a painted wood barge with a dragon's head prow, bobbing in its slip. Three bridges now link the right bank of Hue to the former imperial citadel across the water. Two-thirds of Hue's population of 200,000 live on the citadel side.

Spoiled by five days of imported luxuries at the Metropole, I found my room depressing. In the bathroom, a rusted shower head and drain were set in the broken tiles next to the toilet. Near the bed, a nightstand held one complimentary tea bag and two cups, to go with the battered Chinese hot water thermos. A huge pair of old rubber thongs, the inner soles discolored by sweat stains, had been stacked with care against an armoire for my comfort and relaxation. Clearly the humongous sandals had not been made for Vietnamese feet; for all I knew, they could have been holdovers from the American era. I learned the next day that the hotel had begun life in 1961 as a business venture launched by

Madame Nhu, the beautiful, Frenchified sister-in-law of Ngo Dinh Diem. That may have explained the bad vibes. Shortly after its grand opening the hotel had become a fortified officers' compound.

Of all the idiocies we perpetrated on South Vietnam, as opposed to the outright horrors, the worst idiocy of all, because of its supreme insensitivity, colossal ignorance, and callous disregard for the deep-rooted culture, was the installation of a reclusive, mystical Catholic to represent a Buddhist nation. Diem was the handpicked choice of Cardinal Spellman, who'd met him at a Maryknoll seminary in Ossining, New York. His younger brother, Ngo Dinh Nhu, emerged as the real man with the power, running the secret police and the strategic hamlets program, a Kennedy counterinsurgency scheme that relocated peasants into barbed-wire compounds to keep them safe for democracy. An older brother was the archbishop of Hue. Madame Nhu stepped onto the international stage as the unmarried Diem's official hostess. She also took it upon herself to dictate fashions and morals during the Ngo family's reign.

From New York I'd put in a formal request to visit Dieu De Pagoda. First thing in the morning, Tra took us there, rather proud that he'd understood my message. He knew it, he said, as the National Pagoda.

Dieu De stands just outside the imperial citadel, a squat grey stone structure with a spacious courtyard and four low towers—nothing you'd go out of your way to see if you hadn't gotten stuck on one vivid moment in Vietnamese history. If you hadn't remembered the monks consumed by orange flames, if you hadn't recalled the face of Thich Tri Quang.

Hue's temples and pagodas had been the radiating center of Buddhist opposition to the Diem regime, and two subse-

quent regimes, during the war. From a command post in Dieu
De, the saffron-robed monk Thich Tri Quang—Thich means
"venerable"—had directed the dissident movement, shuttling
between the three southern cities of Hue, Danang, and
Saigon with his placid round face, shaved head, and glowing
eyes. I'd thought of the charismatic young leader in those
days as a calm Yul Brynner with emotional depth.

By reputation the Vietnamese are not a very religious people, or rather, they seem open to many religions and ethical
systems—Confucianism, Taoism, animism, ancestor worship,
Catholicism, the strange sect in the Mekong Delta known as
Cao Dai, even Islam—but when all is said and done, most
Vietnamese are Buddhists. While the orderly rites of Confucianism historically reflected the authoritarian traditions in
Vietnamese thinking, antihierarchical Buddhism, with its
smoking incense pots, tinkling bells, and barefoot mendi-
cants, was the common folk's religion. Mahayana, a gaudy,
outward-looking strain of the faith, had flowered in the heart
of mandarin Hue.

Diem had not only filled all his key government posts with
Catholics and awarded them the choicest real-estate and
business deals, he had banned the public display of Buddhist
banners. At first the Buddhists began organizing simply to
regain religious parity within their country. In May 1963 the
monks of Hue organized a celebration of the Buddha's birth-
day. Nine people were killed when government soldiers fired
into the crowd. The brothers Diem and Nhu tried to blame
the Viet Cong.

One month later, Thich Quang Duc, a senior monk from
Thien Mu Pagoda near Hue, got out of a car at a busy intersection in Saigon and assumed the prayerful lotus position
while his fellow bonzes poured gasoline over his robes and
head. Lighting a match, Quang Duc set himself on fire. As

the terrible orange flames consumed the orange robes and the body toppled over into a charred heap, one of the attending bonzes called through a bullhorn in Vietnamese and English, "A Buddhist priest burns himself to death, a Buddhist priest becomes a martyr." Pictures of the immolation appeared in our newspapers the next morning. Tri Quang had alerted Malcolm Browne of the Associated Press.

Three more monks and a nun immolated themselves in August. That was when Madame Nhu called the pyres "a barbecue" and added, "Let them burn and we shall clap our hands." Her husband chimed in, "I'll be happy to supply the gasoline." Diem and Nhu staged a military sweep of the pagodas while Washington began casting about for some new miracle men to carry the banner for democracy in South Vietnam. With CIA cooperation Diem and Nhu were assassinated during a generals' coup three weeks before President Kennedy was felled in Dallas. Americans went into mourning, forgetting Vietnam, putting our hopes in the man who was going to heal our national pain. Lyndon Baines Johnson.

Tri Quang's Buddhists had seen their movement as a third force, a "middle way" between the Communist insurgents and the corrupt, interchangeable regimes in Saigon. Surely they were a graceful way out for the Americans, if we had cared to take it. But as hard as the Buddhists tried, they failed utterly and miserably in their attempts to win American support. Diplomats shrank from contact with the militant bonzes, sensing (correctly) that a major thrust of the struggle movement was a reaction against Western ways, putting out the word (falsely) that Tri Quang and his fanatics were really a front for the Viet Cong. In the final analysis, the homegrown Buddhists simply didn't fit into the American agenda. They were too much of a wild card. We went there to fight Communists with arms and technology—and to paraphrase the immortal words of Joseph Stalin, how many divisions did the barefoot bonzes command? So America turned its back on the Buddhists, and in the end many of their secular adherents joined the Viet Cong.

During the spring of 1966, when I was working as a newswriter for ABC-TV in New York, the Buddhists of Hue were back in the news, conducting a hunger strike inside the gates of the U.S. consulate. This time a female nun, Thich Nu Thanh Quang, set herself on fire, in the courtyard of Dieu De Pagoda. Her suicide began another wave of immolations. Sympathetic protest marches erupted in Danang and Saigon, but Hue was in a true state of insurrection. Rioting students burned down the USIS library and set the consulate on fire. And then it was over. Our new man of the hour, the snappy fellow in the neck scarf and aviator goggles, General Nguyen Cao Ky, brutally silenced the pagodas. Hue took more time to suppress than Danang or Saigon; it always did. The raid at Dieu De was especially violent. Close to death from a hunger strike, Tri Quang was spirited away to a Saigon hospital—the generals had not dared to kill him. The Vietnamese Gandhi was quiet for the duration.

A young monk with a curious half-shaved tonsure, the sign of his novitiate, greeted us at Dieu De's entrance and asked us to take off our shoes. Betraying a slight nervousness, or perhaps just an unfamiliarity with his role, he pointed out the sanctuary and altars—just what you'd expect from a church sexton anywhere in the world, except that this was the Socialist Republic of Vietnam, so the subtext was more interesting. The nervous young man had chosen a path for himself that was far from mainstream.

I scanned a row of framed black-and-white portraits on the wall, searching for Tri Quang's, knowing I'd recognize that

Yul Brynner face in a flash. He wasn't there. The chilling
thought occurred to me that he had been obliterated,
become a non-person. I remembered later that pictures of living monks do not appear on Buddhist altars, but I was entitled to a touch of paranoia. The last word I'd been able to
find on Tri Quang was a terse remark in Stanley Karnow's
1983 *Vietnam: A History* that he'd been banished to a distant
monastery when the Communists took over in 1975.

With the earnest novice hurrying behind, I poked into
recesses, down corridors, following the unmistakable sound of
chanting. Peering through a half-closed door, I found the
source. A dozen brown-robed monks, their shaved heads covered by brown wool-knit watch caps in the morning cold,
were singing in response to the readings of a wizened master.
Two nuns in grey sat slightly apart.

I ran to get Maggie. Rude, rude Americans, we went
around to a side window for a better view. The class broke up
a few minutes later. Apparently our rudeness paid off; the
monks were happy to talk with us. They were from Thien Mu
Pagoda. Three mornings a week they traveled to the city to
study the sutra with Dieu De's master.

It may be hard to faze a monk in general, and it may be
even harder to faze a monk from Hue. While Maggie took
pictures, I casually asked after Tri Quang. I didn't feel casual,
I felt daring. But the question seemed no more momentous to
the brown-cassocked monks than if I'd asked, "And how's
Cousin Joe?"

"Tri Quang," nodded the monk with the best command of
English. "Tri Quang is very well. He is living at the An
Quang Pagoda in Saigon."

A flickering newsreel unrolled from a dim recess in my
brain. Saigon's militant pagoda during the sixties. Tri Quang's
home base in that city. I had typed the words "An Quang

Pagoda" many times in the sixties, but I'd read that it had been destroyed in the later stages of the war.

Politely, I pressed the monk. "An Quang Pagoda is still standing?"

"Of course."

"And if I go there, will I be able to see Tri Quang?"

The monk shook his head. "Tri Quang lives as a hermit. He sees no one but monks from Hue."

"But why?"

"He says he has completed his role in history."

After the puzzling encounter at Dieu De, we entered the imperial citadel through the restored Noon Gate. The moment remains a blur for me, for that's where I confronted a fact of modern life that I wasn't prepared for, and that I tried to push out of my mind for the rest of my time in the city.

A man, a beggar, suddenly emerged from behind a pillar, carrying a pale child about three years old who appeared to be weaving in and out of consciousness. He offered her to us in a mute appeal. The right side of the child's face from her temple to her cheek bore the clean, healing marks of recent wounds. They had probably been inflicted by a wooden mallet, a meat tenderizer to judge from the pattern of the sharp, neat holes.

I don't recall how long we stood there, frozen in a mute tableau, before the man broke the horrible spell by moving away. Later that evening, when we found the words to discuss what we'd seen, neither Maggie nor I had any doubt that human hands had caused the child's wounds. The man holding her may or may not have been her father, he may or may not have wielded the mallet, but one thing was certain. He was using the abused child to attract sympathy and money.

What I saw at Noon Gate was an isolated occurrence. Although hawkers and beggars pursued us with Dickensian insistence quite often in Hue and elsewhere in Vietnam, we never encountered another child who'd been deliberately abused. Still, the sheer number of beggars, especially child beggars, was disturbing. For reasons I don't altogether fathom, our guides never interfered when we were surrounded and besieged by unwanted attention. I suspect that the sight of human misery and its calculated flaunting to earn a living off tourist guilt was par for the course as far as they were concerned, and they may have been curious to see how we'd react. We reacted, as the trip progressed, by becoming inured and cynical. Then that phase passed and was replaced by a more selective response. I saw no distended stomachs in Vietnam, as one might in Somalia, for example, but the hard reality of life is that half of the children and many adults are malnourished. According to statistics from Save the Children and from development studies sponsored by the World Bank, one out of three Vietnamese children suffers from second- or third-degree malnutrition. Sometimes it's seasonal, as in rural villages that live from one rice harvest to the next, and sometimes it's chronic. More than half the farmers in central Vietnam, and perhaps 20 percent in the north's Red River Delta, eat less than fifteen hundred calories a day, substantially below the requirements suggested by the World Health Organization.

What I didn't know at the time, but what I learned subsequently in conversations with some Vietnamese writers, is that there has been much earnest debate in Vietnamese newspapers about the increasing countrywide phenomenon of beggars and begging. With a spirited passion for analysis, my writer friends were quick to categorize four kinds of beggars: those who are unable to work, those who are lazy, those who follow the customs of their village (there are some villages where by tradition everyone goes out on the road to beg for one month out of the year), and those who are just plain poor and needy.

When a traveler is surrounded by a band of children who are begging but who are also making a *game* of begging, as children tend to do, it's hard to evaluate the level of need versus the pesky level of play. Neither can an individual stand on a street corner with an open pocketbook to correct an endemic social wrong such as hunger. I took to carrying some small notes, three-hundred- and five-hundred-dong denominations, the equivalent of a few pennies, for the particularly winsome kids and old people who got to my heart.

Hue's imperial citadel dates from 1802, when a southern Nguyen armed by the French defeated his northern Trinh rivals, uniting the two halves of Vietnam for the first time in modern history. France got less out of the victory than it had expected, but the Dutch, who'd been backing the Trinhs, were forced to retire from Indochina. Weaker in peace than in warfare, Emperor Gia Long gave annual tribute payments to China and moved his ancestral altars from Saigon to the site of the old Nguyen capital of Phu Xuan, the better to watch over both parts of his kingdom. In consultation with his astrologers and geomancers, he leveled eight villages and began building Hue with conscripted forced labor. His fourth son, Minh Mang, the second emperor at Hue, continued the program of grand construction.

A pretty confection of chinoiserie, the citadel took shape as a nest of three boxes. Its fortified ramparts followed the style of the French military architect Sebastien Vauban; its winged gates, interior palaces, and landscaped gardens were patterned after the Forbidden City of Ming dynasty Peking. Artisans and tradespeople lived in the outer precinct, while the middle enclave was reserved for the mandarin class of scholars and administrators of the royal court. The innermost precinct, the Forbidden Purple City, was for royalty only—the monarch, his family, and the concubines and eunuchs who served at his pleasure. Within its sanctum a rivalrous lot of brothers, nephews, and sons succeeded one another on the throne. After the first seventy years, the Nguyen dynasty was little more than a French charade.

France had already annexed the Mekong Delta, renaming it Cochin China, and was subduing the north, or Tonkin, when a small invasion force broke into the citadel in 1885, burning the university library and sacking the palaces of their gold and silver. From that point on, the power in Hue moved none too subtly across the river, where a French colonial town arose to administer the slice of central Vietnam they called Annam. The conquerors retained the "native" monarchy, efficiently deposing any foolhardy royal successor who stepped out of line, and continuing the policy of conscripting forced labor. Such was the power of colonial rule that the Vietnamese accepted their designation as Annamites or Annamese, terms of contempt borrowed from the Chinese and embraced by the French. The mountain range running down the spine of the country appeared on maps as the Annamite Cordillera; it is now the Truong Son.

The last emperor at Hue was the playboy Bao Dai, who defined for all time what it takes to be a puppet ruler. Bao Dai hunted and disported at the royal resort of Dalat under the French, and scarcely bothered to change his habits under the Japanese. He renounced his crown in 1945 when the Viet Minh declared the national republic, and he reclaimed it, under French prompting, three years later. Bao Dai was deposed for good in 1954 when Diem was installed in the South.

We spent the rest of the morning touring the royal ruins, dogged by vendors offering sheafs of sketches and rubbings that we didn't wish to buy. Great gnarled frangipani trees lined a graceful stone pathway that led to a field where humble sweet potatoes grew on the site of a former palace. Most of the Forbidden Purple City had been bombed into a void during the first Indochina war, when the French and the Viet Minh fought over Hue. During our war, local citizens stripped the surviving palaces of their furniture and tapestries, from the usual motives of poverty, desperation, and greed. Many of the precious art objects ended up abroad.

Except for the flowering frangipanis, a bridge, a pond, and a courtyard with two stone elephants and some undersized stone mandarins, I got the feeling that whatever I was seeing of the citadel's imperial splendors was a restoration.

Americans were so sublimely ignorant of Vietnam when our government decided to wage a war there that few of us had any idea that Tet was the name of the week-long New Year's celebration. Tet heralds the coming of spring, a time for cleaning the house, repaying debts, starting afresh, readying the ancestral altar, cooking special foods, donning new clothes, visiting family and friends, giving gifts. The holiday begins on the first day of the first month of the old lunar calendar—the same new moon that kicks off the Chinese New Year, in late January or early February, with big rounds of firecrackers.

For Tet 1968, the Year of the Monkey, there were rounds of mortars and rockets as Viet Cong sappers and small units of the North Vietnamese Army staged coordinated strikes against dozens of supposedly impregnable targets across the South. The battle for Hue was the bloodiest of all. Before dawn on January 31, NVA artillery began pounding the city, catching its ARVN defenders off guard. By daylight, the populace on both sides of the river could see the Viet Cong flag on the citadel's highest tower. The flag was to stay there for twenty-five days before U.S. Marines, backed by air strikes and navy gunfire, recaptured the city in street-to-street fighting. The marine counter-assault began on the right bank and crossed into the citadel. By the time an American flag was hoisted over the ramparts, half of Hue had been flattened and ten thousand lay dead.

Tet was the emotional turning point for most Americans back home, the moment when the credibility gap widened into a chasm. At a bitter sacrifice of their most dedicated fighters—the greater part of the South's Viet Cong infrastructure died in the offensive—the Communists proved not only that they weren't "finished" but that the light at the end of the tunnel was theirs. But the cost was too high. The audacious campaign was a mission of suicidal intensity, the only tactic that could possibly work against the technological superiority of the American forces, but it had been launched in the expectation that the South would rise up in a great popular insurrection. Instead, most of the civilian population burrowed into itself or tried to flee, as it always did when the fighting came to its door. In Hue, Vietnamese civilians suffered the highest casualties of the Tet Offensive. It still isn't certain how many were killed by American firepower and how many by the insurgents, who rounded up known collaborators and settled old scores.

Today, through UNESCO headquarters in Paris, the French are spearheading a restoration of some of the former imperial dwellings from old aerial maps and sketchy architectural drawings. The uphill project has proceeded in fits and starts, on very limited funds. On the day we were touring, two local workmen on scaffolds were applying gilt paint to a circular column inside a pavilion. Hue deserves all the international aid it can get, and it seems heartless to quarrel with UNESCO's well-meaning gesture, but the restoration struck me as a great waste of money in the context of Vietnam's human needs. UNESCO's intention, of course, is to bring tourists to Hue, as well as to give local artisans a make-work project. I happen to love ruins. I can spend days ruminating happily among ancient stones and glyphs, trying to comprehend the mysteries of lost civilizations, but the more I saw of Hue's nineteenth-century ruins, the less impressive I found them. They simply weren't old enough to inspire flights of fancy or admiration. Apparently I'm not the only one who thinks so. International donors have been slow to respond to UNESCO's calls for help in the Hue restoration.

The cuisine of Hue redeemed itself at Dzach Lau at 23 Ben Nghe, on the right bank of the river, in a real neighborhood house that looked like a French bungalow. Dzach Lau, with a *z* to tell you how to pronounce the *d*, is a colloquial expression for "Number One." It sure was.

Dzach Lau's proprietor was an ethnic Chinese chef who had presided over the Huong Giang's kitchen during the war. He opened his own restaurant in 1975. Our waiters, two brothers, had been ARVN soldiers. According to the chef, business was slow. I believed him. We were his only customers. We ate on the porch, choosing "rocket shrimp" from the menu. Stuffed with pork, onions, and mushrooms, their little tails sticking out of the edible rice paper wrapping, the shrimp did look like rockets. Sweet potatoes were on my mind since we'd just walked through a field of them in the bombed-out Forbidden Purple City. The chef happily french-fried a delectable batch at my request. After the sumptuous lunch, we took a tour of the house and met the chef's extended family. Stepping over a live fish quivering on the kitchen floor, I couldn't have cared less whether Dzach Lau would have passed a New York restaurant inspection. The meal and the welcome were fantastic.

That afternoon and the following day we drove to several imperial tombs on the outskirts of the city. While the Western powers were insinuating themselves into Vietnam, the Nguyen emperors employed vast armies of conscripts in necropolis building. The tombs were a lot more than tombs; they were royal resorts set in landscaped parks, inspired, as the citadel had been inspired, by the glories of Peking under the Mings.

The last tomb on our list had been constructed during the 1920s as the final resting place of Khai Dinh, Bao Dai's sickly father. Its interior galleries were encrusted from floor to ceiling with fragments of porcelain and colored glass painstakingly assembled into roses, trees, lotus blossoms, bunches of grapes—a rococo style of mosaic inlay that most people would find screamingly excessive on a fake Tiffany lampshade. In the center of this mad extravaganza, a life-size replica of Khai Dinh was seated on a gilt throne. Guy wires held a weighty bronze canopy adorned with ceramic tassels above his head. You had to admire the engineering feat, if nothing else.

By then, Maggie and I had had more than enough of mausoleums. As parks, the sites of the tombs were beautiful, with rolling green hills, man-made lakes, and manicured pine forests, yet they were curiously devoid of people. No lovers holding hands, no families on picnics.

"Tell me honestly, Tra, what do you think of these imperial tombs?"

We were sitting at an empty gazebo built over a lake at Tu Duc's tomb. The emperor had come here to fish and write poetry in 1883 while French warships were sailing up the Perfume River. UNESCO had rebuilt the gazebo in 1984.

"What do you think I think?" Tra responded. "I think these tombs are very beautiful."

"They make me unhappy, Tra. All this ostentatious display of wealth that was robbed from the people."

He brightened. "Yes, but now the tombs belong to the people."

"Then why don't the people come here?"

"The people are too busy working," he answered stiffly.

Hue has a big unemployment problem, but I let his comment slide.

Just then two Canadian backpackers arrived at the gazebo, accompanied by two Hue University students they'd met in town. The induced inertia of the guided tour was getting to me. "You're allowed to fraternize with Westerners?" I asked one of the students.

He smiled broadly, with a wink at Tra. "Oh, sure. For the last two years it's been okay to talk to foreigners."

Tra didn't smile back. Instead he retreated with Mr. Kha to the gazebo's far end. Before I butted in, the students had been telling the Canadians how difficult it was to meet young women. A real conversation.

"May I ask," I intruded again, "did you learn your English at the university?"

My question produced a roar. "We learned our English by cassette," said one. "At the university we studied Russian for four years." They glanced over at Tra, their designated symbol of the government system.

Our voices must have carried through the empty park, for soon we were joined by a young man who was peddling silk paintings. "The artist is my brother," the new fellow volunteered without conviction.

"See what I mean?" said one of the students, exchanging a significant look with the Canadians. The paintings were schlock.

Undeterred by the cool welcome, the peddler knelt on the planked floor, spreading his wares. Politely I riffled through the hastily made designs. A bird on a branch, a boat on a river. There was nothing I cared to buy.

"Tell your guides to take you to Hue's slums," one of the students called out when we left the gazebo. "They never show you that."

In the evening I went out in search of an independent adventure, getting no farther than the Hotel Hue, the new place on Le Loi Boulevard next door to our hotel. One look at the jumping lobby and I knew that the Hotel Hue had drained off the tourists from the former enterprise of Madame Nhu.

Two Americans were tying a load on in the dining room. I joined them.

"We're here on a vacation," Bob said, trying to catch the waiter's eye.

"That's what he says. This is our midlife crisis."

"Don't listen to him. He's my best friend in the world, but he's a great kidder. Hey, is that waiter avoiding me, or what?"

"Let me ask you something," said Harry. "They're so industrious, so why are they so poor? They've got the fourth largest standing army in the world, that's why. Screw it. No Americans are going to make it here but big corporations."

"Harry's upset because he bought a bottle of Stolichnaya vodka in Hanoi."

"Yeah. I bought a bottle of rice wine. It had the seal on it, for chrissake."

"So what did you expect for two dollars?"

"If they're so fucking clever, why are they so poor?"

"You answered that one already."

"You know something, I felt sorry for them when I got here."

"Now he's feeling sorry for himself."

"This is serious, Bob. You notice how they tell you the Americans bombed this and the Americans bombed that? We weren't the only ones who destroyed this country."

After a while I moved to another table. Declan and Annie were British. They worked in Saudi Arabia at the King Khalid Hospital in Jedda. He purchased equipment, she was a nurse. Jedda was their way of seeing the world and making some money.

"So what's your impression of Hue?"

"Hue is in trouble," said Declan. "Hue is a city of the past. I think we arrived seventy years too late."

"Thank you," I said. "I'm writing that down."

The next day we hired a private motorized sampan to take us up the Perfume River to the Thien Mu Pagoda. The boat's owners were a husband-and-wife team who'd borrowed a thousand dollars to make the payment. Their skin was nut-brown, off the color chart of Hue's typical range of complexions. As soon as we were underway, the wife showed us their year-old baby. Then she disappeared into the cabin. I thought that was it for the trip, but she returned after a while with a pot of tea.

We sat on a bamboo mat and drank tea. Out of respect for the boat we had removed our shoes. It was drizzling slightly. Maggie dozed off. Tra and Mr. Kha dozed off. While the boat husband steered, the boat wife crept over to where I was sitting.

She pointed to the ends of my hair where I still had a permanent. I nodded. She pointed to her own permed hair. I nodded some more. We giggled. Moving in closer, the boat wife pointed to my white leg with its trace of dark hair. I countered with an open-palm gesture meaning "That's life" and pointed to her hairless brown leg. She responded with a shrug, her own "That's life."

With the introductions out of the way, I offered her a Carlton, pantomiming furiously, "This cigarette's a tough draw, you're not going to like it." Inhaling deeply, she frowned in agreement and quickly mimed, "But I admire your lighter." I gave her my lighter.

My pen and notebook were lying in my lap. She admired the pen. My favorite purple lighter, my best pen. I mimed, "This is a very good pen, I really don't want to part with it," and handed it over.

The boat wife pantomimed, "Yes, this is a very good pen indeed," and cheerfully stuck it in her pocket.

When Maggie woke up, the boat wife left my side to pantomime her admiration for Maggie's silver-and-turquoise ring. No dice. The ring stayed put on the photographer's finger.

We gave the enterprising pair a lavish tip when they let us off at the Thien Mu Pagoda. They were engaging people.

There have been, on my travels, a few world-renowned places where, from the moment I set foot on the soil, I understood on a visceral level why *this precise spot*, not the one down the road, had been chosen as sanctified ground. Perching on the Sibyl's Rock in Delphi, wandering through the streets of old Jerusalem, I felt the power, the peace, the elevated sense of well-being. Every fiber of my body announced that I was treading on a holy place. Since there isn't a grain of spirituality in my bones, I attribute the phenomenon to a practical and definable confluence of geographic and atmospheric conditions. The ancients who settled these places, who fought over them time and again, staked out their claims for a reason. Something about the lay of the land, the mountain, the sea, the valley, the barometric pressure, heightened their perceptions and deepened their feelings.

That's how I felt at Thien Mu Pagoda.

According to legend, the Vietnamese are descended from dragons and fairies. In the legend of Thien Mu, a fairy woman appeared to a Nguyen warlord in 1601 and told him to build a pagoda on a hill above the Perfume River. Some say the fairy came to the warlord in a dream. Others say the warlord was taking an evening stroll on the hill when he encountered an old lady swathed in red and green raiments who announced, "This hill deserves a temple," and then vanished into the clouds.

In any event, a Cham tower once stood on the hillock, and the first Thien Mu Pagoda was built from Cham bricks. The pagoda was destroyed and rebuilt many times over the next two centuries while the Trinhs and the Nguyens fought over the central plains. The present seven-story octagonal tower, beautifully proportioned, was constructed in 1844 during the six-year reign of the emperor Thieu Tri. Under Thieu Tri, Vietnam entered a great period of expansion, annexing the watery lands of the Mekong Delta that had belonged to the kingdom of Cambodia. He died at the age of forty, supposedly of apoplexy induced by an erroneous report of a French invasion.

We disembarked onto a wood dock in sight of the tower and climbed the hillock, passing a clutch of refreshment stands whose sole refreshment was ripe green bananas. It turned out that there was a lot more to Thien Mu Pagoda than its emblematic tower. The monastery's well-tended grounds and outbuildings stretched invitingly before us. Lavender orchid vines clambered over a latticework trellis. A bonsai collection of miniature pines, ficus, and tea trees flourished in ceramic jardinieres. I was admiring the bonsai when a well-dressed Vietnamese woman stepped up to ask in English, "How much do you think they would cost in America?"

"Oh, I don't know. A hundred, two hundred dollars?"

She frowned. "I think more than that."

We were discussing the relative prices and merits of bonsai when a small brigade of brown-robed monks carrying hoes over their shoulders marched past in single file, a picturebook vision of the Seven Dwarfs returning from the fields.

"Maggie, get the monks!"

I was sorry as soon as the words flew out of my mouth. Back in Hanoi the photographer had made it abundantly clear that she didn't appreciate such lightning effusions, which sounded to her like peremptory orders. This time my voice had been loud enough to attract the monks' attention. One of them waved as he disappeared around a corner. He was one of the monks we had met the day before at Dieu De.

There was a modern shrine at Thien Mu, the British Austin that had carried Thich Quang Duc to Saigon in 1963. It stood in an open shed. Someone had taped Malcolm Browne's photo of the immolation to the inside of the windshield. I watched Maggie adjust the lens on her Leica before I returned to the bonsai pavilion. Tra and Mr. Kha had absented themselves, probably to give us some freedom.

I wandered around for a while on my own and then walked back to Maggie, calling her name. She was lying across the hood of the car. Tears streamed down her face. "Leave me alone, leave me alone. Just go away."

It was her moment to surrender to Vietnam's sorrow, to get

some of the pain out of her system. I wandered off again by myself. The novice from Dieu De materialized at my side. We strolled in silence through a neatly tended vegetable patch. To my surprise, he took one of my cigarettes. With great effort he began speaking.

"I am a Buddhist monk."

"Yes."

"Buddhists do not eat meat."

"No."

"We do not have women."

"No." I couldn't help myself. "But you do smoke cigarettes. Why is that?"

He shook off my impertinence and pressed on. "We grow our own vegetables, but we *cannot* grow our own rice!" He was looking at me for some kind of confirmation. Agitated, he repeated, "*We cannot grow our own rice, but we can grow everything else.*"

I pondered the point he wished me to understand. It took me a while to get it. In my Vietnam time warp, I'd been re-creating the Buddhists of the sixties. The novice was making me confront a more recent reality. After the Communists took over the South, organized Buddhism had been repressed yet again. Apparently this time around, the monks had been called parasitic for relying on the peasants to feed them.

"No," I said finally. "I guess you can't be expected to grow your own rice."

Maggie joined us, dry-eyed and quiet. Another of the monks from Dieu De, the good English speaker, drifted over, sandals flopping. He swirled his brown cassock, he tugged at his brown watch cap. I recalled from my hiking days that 30 percent of the body's heat escapes from the head. The percentage must be higher if the head is shaved.

The four of us sat on a stone bench facing the planted

fields and a distant tree line. Suddenly the sun broke through the clouds. A feeling of great calm descended on me. Thien Mu was so beautiful. I understood why these young men would renounce the world to spend the rest of their lives on its sacred grounds. Thien Mu was so profoundly peaceful that a monk would travel to Saigon in an Austin and set himself on fire to preserve the tradition.

"Tell me again, how long did the recent bad times for Buddhists last?"

"From 1975 to 1985," the monk in the watch cap said quickly.

"Well, I think you're home free. If you'll forgive me for saying this, you are now an important tourist attraction. The government needs you."

"Do you trust your guides?"

The question and its intensity caught me by surprise.

"Yes, I do. Of course I do."

"We think they are police."

"They're not police." I stifled a laugh. "Maybe at one time guides were police, but not now. I really don't think so. I think they're just guides."

He made a sour face. There was no use in debating the point. For the moment I squelched my loyalty to Tra and Mr. Kha.

At the monks' invitation we repaired to their quarters for tea. I removed my shoes, feeling honored. Boy novices with their off-putting tonsures were chopping vegetables in the kitchen. We sat at a bare wood table. I took in the ubiquitous Chinese thermos, the tiny, cheap modern cups. The sole decoration on the wall was a kitschy embossed print of a kitten.

Why a kitten? Why the repeated suppression of Buddhists? I knew the answer to that one. These stubborn, implausible Buddhists would throw a wrinkle into any authoritarian regime. "The Communists always want to be a mass organization, but Buddhism *is* the mass," Tri Quang once said in the sixties.

The monk in the watch cap wrote his name and address in my notebook, preceded by "Buddhist monk," in case I forgot. Then the novice took us outside to look for our guides. I gave him the rest of my pack of cigarettes. Maggie promised to send her pictures.

"*Chao.*"

"*Chao.*"

I had started to walk down the path when the monk in the watch cap called to me urgently. I followed him back into the pavilion. His eyes darted left and right. Reaching into his brown robes, he pulled out two envelopes. "Would you mail these letters when you get home?"

"Of course!" I jammed the envelopes into my pants pocket. I was an eager conspirator but a clumsy one. "Oh! I shouldn't have folded them!"

"That's all right. You had to, to fit into your pocket."

"It will be two weeks before I can mail these."

"That's okay."

We repeated our intense goodbyes.

The monk's envelopes burned like hot coals in my pocket as we drove back to the city. "Hue is still quite a Buddhist stronghold, isn't it, Mr. Kha?"

Tra turned to stare at me. Mr. Kha giggled. "Yes. A stronghold."

I mailed the monk's letters the day after I got back to New York. Only then did I look at the names and addresses: a monk in Australia and a monk in Falls Church, Virginia. Airmail postage is very expensive in Vietnam, and letters can take months to reach their destination. I think that's what my conspiratorial mission was about. But I also believe that the monk from Thien Mu didn't trust the postal service to process a letter without scanning its contents.

Now, why a kitten?

The more I thought about the kitten, the more I began to recall other Communist countries I'd visited, where places of worship kept a picture of the state's paramount leader on the wall, just to be on the safe side. In the following months, news filtered out from Hue about the arrest and conviction of several Thien Mu monks charged with "instigating civil disorder" at a public protest. They wanted religious control of their own Unified Buddhist Church, and the return to them of the nationalized pagodas.

It is a day for conspiracies and rebellions.

"Tra! Since we got to Hue we've met nobody but monks and tourists."

"Tra! Last night the French tour group went to a dance performance. Why didn't we know about it?"

"Tra! I hate the Huong Giang Hotel. I want to switch over to the Hotel Hue."

"Tra! We're isolated over here. Is there a guesthouse on the citadel side of the river?"

The guide from Danang stares moodily out the car window.

"Well, the least you can do," I say tartly, "is take us to the university."

"No."

"What do you mean, no?"

"You did not request permission to visit the university."

"Tra, how could I have known in New York that I had to make a request to see the university?"

"So go to the university! You can walk from the hotel."

"But I need a translator." This said in a whine.

Mr. Kha intervenes in Vietnamese. Tra leaves the car. Cung drives us to the university. First to a teacher's college, and then, after asking directions from some friendly students, down Le Loi Boulevard with its pollarded trees to the university proper, a ramshackle, old-fashioned red-brick complex that used to be a Catholic school.

Instantly I get my bearings. Grounds, buildings, connecting paths. A portico with rows and rows of bike racks. It's 5:00 p.m. We're just in time to see a mass exodus of students heading for their bikes. Oh no.

"Hello! We're Americans. We've come to see your university."

The tactic works like a charm. Students gather around us at the bike racks.

"You're from *America?*"

"Yes. I was hoping to see a class in session, but it looks like you're all going home."

"There is a class now in that building."

"There is?"

"Yes. An English class."

"An English class? *Maggie!* There's an English class in that building! Will you show us the way? Mr. Kha, Mr. Kha, we're going to a classroom!"

"Please, please! You must wait. First I must ask the gate-keeper for permission."

"Maggie, let's go!"

Leaving Mr. Kha to negotiate with the college gatekeeper, we run ahead. Up a flight of creaking wood stairs. Halfway down a narrow corridor. Within minutes Maggie and I are peering through a doorway. About thirty students are hunched over yellowing copies of an old British text. Their young teacher is at the blackboard, tapping with her pointer at the day's lesson: MY FATHER IS A COAL MINER. HIS LIFE IS HARD.

I repeat my greetings. "Hello! We're Americans. We've come to Hue to see your university."

Openmouthed stares. The teacher collects herself quickly. "My students have not had the opportunity to hear an American speak English."

"Ah! I happen to speak English very well."

The students giggle. The teacher invites me to address the class.

Oh. Now I've done it. "Students, I think what we'll do is, uh, I'll speak very slowly. You ask me whatever questions you want and I'll answer them. Okay?"

Glory be. They begin to ask questions. At least the young men do; the young women hang back. (What else is new all over the world?)

"Why did you come to Vietnam?"

"Is this your first visit to our country?"

"Do you like Hue?"

I'm warming to the task, encouraging their questions, enunciating in a pedagogical manner, when I hear a commotion down the hall. What is it? Police? An armed guard?

It's Mr. Kha. "Maggie, Susan, we must leave immediately! We don't have permission!"

We depart as abruptly as we arrived, leaving a classroom of students to fill in the puzzle.

"The gatekeeper," Mr. Kha apologizes as we head for the car. "He was afraid he would get into trouble. He telephoned the administrator, I heard him do it. The administrator asked if you had permission. The administrator was afraid that *he* would get into trouble."

"It's okay, Mr. Kha. The same thing might happen in the

United States. You can't just go barging into classrooms." I break into uncontrollable laughter. "Mr. Kha, you were terrific. You stalled the gatekeeper just long enough."

Our man from Hanoi grins.

One of Ho Chi Minh's farseeing visions was to place national literacy on an equal footing with the fight against foreign invaders and famine. In 1945, on the very first school day of the newly declared independent Vietnam, he addressed a letter to the nation's students predicting that Vietnam's future depended upon their achievements in learning. Earlier Confucian traditions had inspired the Vietnamese with a great respect for education, but beyond Confucius and Ho, there seem to have been certain indelible traits in the Vietnamese character that made them a verbal, highly articulate people with a passion for spoken poetry and knowledge. Grand artistic endeavors that took shape as ornately carved towers and temples were the chief means of creative expression, ten centuries ago, of their neighbors the Khmers and the Chams, but the Vietnamese, who showed little interest and not much originality in the plastic arts, got hooked on words and the soulful satisfactions of language rhythms. Long epic narratives were committed to memory, everyday speech was infused with poetic allusion.

Vietnam's largely oral tradition was perpetuated under colonial rule, when 90 percent of the population was illiterate, and *kept* illiterate, as Vietnam's present leaders put it, by the French tutelage system. The facts speak eloquently. A 1939 survey found only three hundred college graduates in the entire country. Vietnam, Laos, and Cambodia shared the one university in Indochina (it was in Hanoi), and a minuscule elite enjoyed educational opportunities in Paris.

Quoc ngu, the roman-alphabet writing system invented by

foreign missionaries, became the great enabler when the Viet Minh conducted mass literacy campaigns in the 1940s and 1950s as an intrinsic part of colonial resistance. During the American war, formal education was interrupted by necessity but not forgotten. Schools with a military and Marxist slant were set up in areas the Viet Cong controlled, while soldiers of the North Vietnamese Army were encouraged, even expected, to write letters and keep diaries as a human life-line. Indeed, the most poignant part of the ninety miles of captured and microfilmed North Vietnamese Army documents in the national archives in Washington is the trove of personal diaries in which ordinary foot soldiers scrawled fragments of poetry and confided their hopes and fears. (In the summer of 1993, a copy of these documents was returned to Hanoi.)

With the two halves of Vietnam divided by war and pursuing different forms of nation building, the pattern of acquiring an advanced degree abroad took on an imposed regional difference. While the door remained open to France in the South, fresh opportunities arose in the United States. The irony today is palpable as some of the best modern scholarship on Vietnam now comes from a handful of exiled academics at American and Canadian universities who return to their country of birth on yearly field trips, and to catch up on relatives they left behind. Meanwhile, in the North, scholars were sent to the Eastern-bloc countries and Cuba, and teachers from those countries were seeded in Hanoi.

After Reunification in 1975, Northern cadres descended upon Hue and Saigon primed with their political mission to "reeducate" teachers from the old regime and purge them of their "backward" thinking. Between the chilling effect of such intellectual intimidation and the loss of the scholars who remained abroad, the South underwent a terrible brain drain. Some fifteen years later, the educational system in the North was thrown into roiling upheaval after the collapse of the Soviet Union. Not only was there a sudden budget crunch, but the entire curriculum, from science and technology to economics and language training, was called into question. At Hanoi's Foreign Languages College, to give one example, three-quarters of the four thousand enrolled students summarily switched to the study of English. At this writing, the redundant professors who were trained to teach Russian, Bulgarian, Rumanian, and the like are still carried on staff, although there are few calls for their expertise.

Compared to other Third World countries, literacy rates in Vietnam today are astounding. More than 85 percent of the population can read, and nearly as many can write. The down side is that the public education system is eroding at an alarming pace as the government finds itself shorter and shorter on funds to finance its programs. Tuition fees have been introduced, and enrollment has fallen off from the primary school to the university level.

With unemployment at 20 percent and available jobs mainly in the category of unskilled labor, Vietnam's rice farmers hold the distinction of being the best educated in the world. In what has to be seen as an inevitable corollary, the present generation of college-trained Vietnamese is severely disaffected. Teachers' salaries are absurdly low, lagging behind the cost of living to such an extent that dedicated educators are required to moonlight or to depend on charity from their relatives abroad. Students have suffered a crisis of faith as they see that a diploma is no guarantee of employment. I learned in Hanoi that when the Metropole sent out a hiring call prior to its grand reopening, it was flooded with graduates holding advanced degrees, mostly from the language institutes, who were willing to take any position.

One avenue of study in which there is a dire and acute shortage of trained scholars is the law. A tardy bloomer in a field that many in the Western world consider a blight, Hanoi got around to setting up its first law college in 1979, thirty-four years after Ho Chi Minh announced the formation of a college of archeology. At the time, the priorities were not as skewed as they now seem, since the Communist Party ruled by the simple expedient of issuing administrative decrees and local cadres carried out the orders. Only lately, as the National Assembly has wrested legislative powers from the Party, and as the country as a whole begins to woo foreign business, does the shortage of lawyers, administrative codes, and trained court personnel loom as a crisis.

On our own again for dinner, Maggie and I decide to give the hotel dining room another try. The fresh crab-and-asparagus soup is delicious. So much for first impressions of the Huong Giang's cuisine.

We're tearing into our chicken, discussing the day's events, when I spy an eavesdropper at the next table. From his bulk and the way he's polishing his plate, I take him for a tourist. Korean, I decide. At my invitation, he joins us. He isn't Korean. He's Vietnamese, a journalist from Saigon, on his way to visit his mother in Quang Tri province.

"Quang Tri," I say. "We're going there tomorrow."

After we introduce ourselves he drops a bombshell. He worked for the Associated Press in the last months of the war. Within seconds he and Maggie are trading names of people they know in common. Even I get into the act, mentioning ABC correspondents I worked with twenty-five years ago. He remembers them all.

Our journalist friend paid dearly for his unlucky career move. A few months after the Communists took Saigon there was a knock on the door. He ended up spending ten years in a labor camp for reeducation. "Hard labor," he says. "Very hard labor. My wife and my brother escaped to the States. When they released me, I had only the clothes on my back."

"What did you do?"

He laughs without mirth. "I drove a cyclo for one year." He says it more bitterly than anything he has said before. I can sense his humiliation. He drove people like me.

"Journalism is what I was trained for. I don't know any other way to earn a living." He pulls out a copy of a Saigon paper, shows us his by-line.

"So you're back on track."

"Freelancing. A weekly paper."

He has things to do. He gets up to leave. Listening to him has been a sobering experience. A few months with AP, ten years in a labor camp. What was his crime?

"The news agency couldn't help you?"

He shrugs.

A little later, when I go to my room, I bump into him leaving his room across the hall.

"What are you doing here?" he demands.

"Going to bed. I'm across the hall here." I show him my key.

He nods, relieved. Just another momentary touch of Vietnam paranoia. We say goodbye again, awkwardly. I don't think he knows I'm still reeling from his story.

As I'm packing for our trip to Quang Tri province, there's a knock on the door. It's the young hall porter with my freshly washed and dried sneakers. My poor old Nikes have never looked so clean. I force some money on the porter. He's reluctant to take it.

It's been an unsettling day.

PARALLEL CROSSINGS

On the road again, heading for what the 1954 Geneva Conference, with no sense of future irony, named the Demilitarized Zone. Cung is driving, with Tra on his right. Wearing his Hanoi business suit (I've never seen him in anything else), Mr. Kha is squeezed in the back seat between Maggie and me. The Americans need to look out the windows.

It's hard to believe, but this two-lane asphalt is National Highway 1. The one and only. There is no National Highway 2. It traverses the length of the country for more than one thousand miles, hugging the coastal plains between the South China Sea and the Truong Son Mountains. The French built the highway to connect Hanoi and Saigon for their military, administrative, and transport convenience; they also put in a single-track rail line that runs parallel to the road. To say "the French built" the road or the rail line, as I've just caught myself doing, is egregious shorthand that obfuscates more than it enlightens. The French built nothing that the Vietnamese didn't pay for through a meticulous tax system and conscripted labor. Bombed in the North by the Americans, sabotaged in the South by the Viet Cong, the narrow-gauge track was pieced together after the war, but a paltry handful of switchbacks and sidings make the train ride in either direction very slow going. If you're lucky, the seven-hundred-mile trip from Hanoi to Saigon takes fifty-two hours.

As usual, we're the only car on the road, passing the occasional logging or produce truck, a lumbering bus, an oxcart, a flotilla of bicycles, swerving to avoid a platoon of ducklings waddling in close formation behind their human mother. In turn we're passed by whizzing scooters. Most often the riders are guys in army fatigues and their girlfriends. Highway 1, I notice, is also a footpath, mostly for women in conical hats who carry their loads on bamboo shoulder poles, the traditional method of overland transportation. Highway 1 is a vast national rice-husking station too. Farmers spread their harvest on big mats to dry in the sun. If the rice is ready, an obliging motorist will do a turn as a thresher. The crunch of the wheels separates the grain from the chaff.

This stretch of highway running north from Hue into Quang Tri province is particularly famous. During the first Indochina war it was christened "The Street Without Joy" by French Legionnaires who were periodically ordered to go out and secure it. Dangerous work. Quang Tri province in those days was thick with Viet Minh guerrillas. Quang Tri was thick with Viet Cong guerrillas during our war twenty years later. It's a rule of warfare that whoever controls the road controls the territory.

As we cruise along, my eyes take in something that my brain needs to process. There's a stunted scrub-grass border between the paving and the sparse tree line. I deduce that the scrawny trees must be postwar plantings. If this were an American road, I wouldn't give the wide setback a second thought; I'd assume that the highway department had been manicuring the shoulders. But that can't be right. Not in Vietnam.

Minutes go by before it dawns on me that I'm witnessing the lasting effects of the Rome plow and a chemical agent. To reduce the likelihood of ambush along South Vietnam's roads and waterways during our war, American engineers bulldozed huge strips of tree cover with Caterpillar tractors fitted with special blades. The tractors were made at a factory in Rome, Georgia. A Rome plow could cut through a tree trunk three feet thick. After the vegetation was cleared, other teams came by to spray herbicides on the bulldozed strips. A quarter of a century later, I can see with my own eyes that the new growth on the sides of Highway 1 is still retarded.

Operation Ranch Hand was the code name for the air force defoliation program. From 1962 to 1972, when an international outcry over chemical warfare forced its termination, Ranch Hand's fixed-wing planes sprayed an estimated twenty million gallons of defoliant over an estimated 10 percent of South Vietnam's land mass to deny the Viet Cong their protective forest cover and food supply. Not counted in those figures is the additional spraying done by the navy along the coastline, by helicopter crews along the roadways, and by GIs with backpack equipment around the perimeters of their base camps. Three of the herbicides were known by their can colors. Agents Orange and White defoliated forests. Agent Blue suppressed cropland and roadside vegetation.

Agent Orange contained dioxin, a contaminant that got into the product during the manufacturing process. Agent Orange is the defoliant we hear about most often in the States because of the class-action suit against the chemical companies filed by American veterans who were exposed to it during their tours of duty and later began coming down with deadly symptoms—nerve damage, cancer, birth defects in their children. The National Academy of Sciences now links three forms of cancer (Hodgkin's disease, non-Hodgkin's lymphoma, soft-tissue sarcoma), a recurring skin rash called chloracne, and a rare liver disease, porphyria cutanea tarda, with Agent Orange exposure. Slow on the uptake, the Veterans Administration is now accepting and processing disability claims.

But people develop terrible health problems in the course of a lifetime—how could the veterans and their doctors say with certainty that what happened to them was caused by Agent Orange? Lethal damage to wildlife from dioxin contamination, and the immediate poisonous effects on humans—skin rash, stomach pains, vomiting, diarrhea—are indisputable. Laboratory experiments on mice offer incontrovertible proof of genetic damage, at least in mice. But how do you design a scientifically impeccable, controlled, and quantified study to assay the genetic effects of high dioxin levels in a human population? That was the question asked by the judge who heard the veterans' case, which was ultimately settled out of court, a frustrating conclusion that left the hard facts in limbo. Still, if American vets believed they could marshal evidence of genetic damage as a result of exposure during a one-year tour in Vietnam, and if the National Academy of Sciences and the Veterans Administration now back them up, what might be the genetic effects in the country of impact, where twenty million gallons of defoliant were sprayed over six million acres in ten years?

During the last decade, small groups of environmental scientists from Sweden and the States have gone to Vietnam on limited funds and a lot of heart, and perhaps an admixture of war guilt, to attempt some Agent Orange investigations. What they came up with was suggestive but not conclusive. To their chagrin and frustration, the scientists received less cooperation from Vietnamese officialdom than they had anticipated, or believed they deserved. Access to heavily bombed and sprayed regions often was denied to them for a variety of stated and unstated reasons: because undetonated shells still littered the landscape, because the deadlands and swamps were malaria havens, because there was ethnic unrest at the moment, or because there were secret reeducation labor camps in the region. Instead, the scientists were encouraged to collect anecdotal information and were taken to Saigon's Tu Du Hospital to view row after row of malformed fetuses in formaldehyde, and to chat with a famous pair of Siamese twins. The twins and the fetuses were compelling symbols of the deadly effects of Agent Orange, but they hardly qualified as scientific proof.

It turned out that Vietnam's scientists and doctors placed a low priority on rigorous, expensive studies of the lasting effects of Agent Orange. They had more pressing national health problems to deal with. Vietnam is an impoverished tropical country beset by malaria, malnutrition, hepatitis B, encephalitis, dengue fever, and parasites, and hampered by a polluted water supply, a Third World sanitation system, and an almost total lack of antibiotics. In contrast to these urgent, overwhelming health and medical concerns, the quest for Agent Orange quantification more than twenty years after the last can was sprayed on a forest is an esoteric pursuit.

Gloomy with thoughts of Agent Orange, I stare out the car window and notice that the terrain has suddenly become bleak and scrubby, choked with white silt.

"Is that from the war?" I whisper. Quang Tri had been bombed and napalmed and defoliated more intensively than any other area in the South, except for the central highlands and some parts of the Mekong Delta.

"Sand and salt marsh," Mr. Kha says with a shrug. "The land is no good here."

"Not from the war?"

"No." He and Tra laugh dryly.

Eager to tap into my own war guilt, I'd forgotten my Vietnam geography lesson. The Red River Delta in the North and the Mekong Delta in the South are Vietnam's two fertile crescents. Nature has not blessed this narrow middle region with rich soil.

"So Quang Tri was always a poor province?"

"Yes," echoes Tra. "A poor province."

I puzzle over the irony. This hardscrabble land had been fought over bitterly in the two Indochina wars. While I'd always known that youths from the poorest strata of American society, rural or working-class and disproportionately black, were the grunts of our war, I hadn't fully understood that their counterparts at the low end of the Vietnamese population, the poorest peasants, suffered the brunt of the unholiest destruction. As if to underline the sorry fact, a Soviet-style war memorial made of reinforced concrete looms into view. I crane my neck at the angular hulk that points toward the sky.

"What does it say, Mr. Kha?"

"What? Oh, the monument. 'The Fatherland Will Not Forget You.'" He translates phlegmatically, for every one of these monuments is chiseled with the same phrase, yet the words go into my heart like a knife blade.

I change the subject. "Tra, today we visit Khe Sanh and the minority village, right?"

"Right. Today we go to Khe Sanh and then I show you the minority village."

"Why are those villagers called the Bru Van Kieu? I mean, why do they have three names?"

"Only two names. Van Kieu. Americans are the only people I have heard say Bru."

"Oh, I see." I really don't see at all. I remember that during the war we called all of Vietnam's ethnic minorities "Montagnards," the French word for mountain people, whether or not they lived in the mountains. The Montagnards were tossed around like footballs. Our Montagnards and their Montagnards. Afterward, when some of them came to the States, their real names began to emerge. Hmong, Muong, Nung—nearly sixty distinctive groupings with their own languages, clothes, and customs. Indigenous ethnic minorities account for 10 percent of Vietnam's population. They've had a rough time, as minorities usually do, wishing to cling to their traditional ways, relocated to less desirable land, encouraged (maybe "forced" is more accurate) to abandon the environmentally destructive slash-and-burn farming by which they have eked out a livelihood for centuries.

"So, Tra, when we visit the Van Kieu, shouldn't we bring them gifts?"

"Yes, you bring them gifts."

"But we don't have any gifts."

"When we get to Dong Ha, I will take you to the market where you buy the gifts. You bring the Van Kieu sugar and salt."

"Really! Sugar and salt!"

Our guide from Danang is smiling. Today and tomorrow will be his show. Furthermore, I'm relieved and pleased that we've reached a working accommodation. It began in the Hue citadel, when I picked up a fallen white blossom, put my nose to its yellow throat, and squealed, "Oooh, frangipani!" Asking me to spell it, Tra had gravely announced, "I will learn from you."

I cringe when I hear the phrase "learn from." I'm allergic to buzz words. "Learn from" is hoary old Maoist sloganeering, an exhortation to the masses to follow an exaggerated, usually apocryphal revolutionary example. "Live like." "Learn from." When Tra said, "I will learn from you," I managed to keep a straight face long enough to answer, "And I will learn from you." To which he responded, "We will learn from each other."

But as a matter of fact, that's what we're doing. Tra and I trade odd scraps of information that we enter with great fanfare in our respective notebooks. I copy down the Vietnamese names of the rivers. He records the "American" names of the flowers. His list now includes frangipani, coreopsis, lotus, chrysanthemum, rose, hibiscus, orchid, marigold, lantana, portulaca. I wish I could identify a beautiful flowering vine that looks like an all-day morning glory and smells exactly like garlic when you crush the lavender blossom. That's what Tra and Mr. Kha call it, the garlic flower.

Mr. Kha is mining another vein of "learn from." He wishes to broaden his knowledge of American slang.

"The expression 'I am hot,'" he says in the car. "Is it true, as I've heard, that when an American woman says, 'I am hot,' she is saying that she wishes to have sex?"

"Mr. Kha!" I exclaim in mock horror. "If an American woman says, 'I am hot,' you had better believe she is talking about the weather!"

"Oh," he says, crestfallen. "I had heard otherwise."

"But on the other hand—" He brightens. From what old hat have I pulled this one? "If an American woman should happen to say, 'I am hot to trot,' then she is saying that she wishes to have sex."

He uncaps his pen. "Trot?"

"Trot. When a horse goes faster than a walk but slower than a gallop."

"Hot to trot! Oh my, that is very good. That is wonderful. Thank you."

Dong Ha, a fishing port that was incorporated into the French network of military fortifications, lies on the south bank of the Cua Viet River. A crenellated blockhouse with a belfrylike tower, circa 1947, still dominates the dilapidated town center. Bernard Fall confessed in his classic *Street Without Joy* that he was an aficionado of these funky observation posts, whose usefulness barely survived their construction. They reminded him of Gary Cooper in *Beau Geste*, or Coop again with Marlene Dietrich in *Morocco*. Of course, those sand-blown figments of Hollywood's imagination had been set in North Africa, that other great swatch of French colonial exploitation, but I can see what he meant. Fall died in 1967 covering a U.S. Marine field action in Quang Tri province. Stepped on a land mine. I wonder what romantic imagery he might have summoned in today's Dong Ha. Besides the French blockhouse, the town center now boasts two U.S. tanks, a forklift, and a cannon.

During the American war, Dong Ha had the dubious honor of being the first sizable town south of the DMZ, within easy range of North Vietnamese artillery fire. Situated at the junction of Highway 1 and Route 9, overlooking two important rivers (the Cua Viet and the Cam Lo), Dong Ha became an air-support control center for raids over the North, and division headquarters for the Third Marines during the presidency of Lyndon Johnson. Under Richard Nixon, Dong Ha was turned over to the ARVNs in accordance with the maybe-yes, maybe-no plan of disengagement euphemistically titled "Vietnamization." By the spring of 1972, Dong Ha was a lonely outpost of the southern republic; the North took most of Quang Tri in their Eastertide offensive. With B-52 support, the South recaptured some territory later that summer, but Quang Tri was never really theirs again. Quang Tri town, the provincial capital, was so totally pulverized that Dong Ha was named the new capital after reunification.

Dong Ha is where we are going to spend the night. Cung parks the car at the tourist office so that Tra can sign off on our all-important permissions. We use the free time to explore the unpaved lanes of the market. It's raining again, the beginning of the monsoon season in this part of the country. Last week, I learned from the journalist in Hue, there had been some serious flooding. I don't see the gunny-sacks of sugar and salt that we're expected to bring to the Van Kieu, but I observe that a number of stalls are selling Seiko and Citizen watches. Imported Japanese watches in this neck of the woods? I replenish my stock of disposable lighters and bargain without success for a box of Chinese coconut cookies. The prices are higher than they were in Hanoi. It's frustrating not to be able to shave a few dong off the asking price, but I rationalize that after all, the Chinese cookies have come a longer distance.

At the stall where I finally break down and buy my cook-ies, the women are all smiles, triumphant. Vietnamese women are irrepressible traders. They have a saying, "Three women and a duck make a market." As the country hurtles toward its market-economy future, I wonder how many women will make the transition from the local town markets to big business and big bucks. Women were effectively shut out of the Communist Party leadership. Now that foreign businessmen are entering the country and making their deals, the women may be shut out again.

My freshly washed sneakers are already muddy when Tra comes to collect us, looking uncharacteristically sheepish. He's got a new fellow with him, a faded peacock, short for a Vietnamese, in a zippered grey windbreaker and the local equivalent of cowboy boots with two-inch heels.

"Duy," the new man says. "Nguyen Thanh Duy."

"*Jouie*," Maggie and I parrot. By my calculation he's a well-preserved sixty despite his shock of thick black hair, but I may be off. I'm not the only one making calculations. Duy is looking us up and down, not bothering to hide his irritation.

"Nobody comes to Quang Tri province," he scoffs. "Only returning veterans wish to come here. Ladies should go to Dalat."

Dalat is the mountain resort farther south where the emperors hunted and disported. Now a honeymooners' retreat, it is known for its pine trees and strawberries. As much as I like strawberries, I decided to forgo Dalat in order to see Khe Sanh and the old DMZ. Of all the big battle sites that burn in my mind—Dak To, Pleiku, Ia Drang, Ashau Valley—Khe Sanh is the one that burns brightest, the one I feel I must visit. I'm about to tell Duy that we aren't ladies, but he has turned his attention to Mr. Kha.

"You are from Vinh?" Murmuring in Vietnamese, he shakes Mr. Kha's hand in condolence.

This is the second time I've seen a special gravity extended to Mr. Kha, whose birthplace on the north-central coast was the capital of Ho Chi Minh's home province, a region of arid soil, harsh winds, torrential rains, and great poverty, known for its militance since the fifteenth century, when Le Loi routed the Chinese invaders. Some of the earliest Communist uprisings in the 1930s took place in Vinh and its environs. Indeed, no other region of Vietnam has been marked so deeply by revolutionary history. Vinh was hit hard by French bombs in the 1950s. Rather than surrender, the Viet Minh burned what remained to the ground. A few years later, angry peasants objecting to the bloody excesses of Communist land reform marched on Vinh in a sort of Kronstadt rebellion (and suffered the same fate as the Kronstadt sailors). Rebuilt in the 1960s as an oil depot and supply port for the Ho Chi Minh Trail, Vinh was obliterated again in the successive waves of

Rolling Thunder and Linebacker. The town's present incarnation was built by the East Germans. To have come from Vinh, and survived it, commands respect.

Duy turns to me once more with a baleful stare and performs another mystifying inspection. "Did you buy your gifts for the Bru Van Kieu?"

"Not yet. We couldn't find any sugar and salt."

"Who told you sugar and salt? You bring the Bru medicine and candy." Impatiently he waves us into the car. "Since I have cleared my schedule," he growls, "I will escort you." He hops into the front seat. Tra squeezes in next to him. We climb into the back. Mr. Kha shifts his weight between us ever so slightly. Our original group of five is in the grips of what is usually referred to as a pregnant pause.

"So!" says Duy. "You wish to see Khe Sanh and a minority village, General Tra?" He has wrapped his arms around Tra's shoulders, smothering him in a bear hug. "*General Tra! What an honor!*"

There is a moment of dead air before Mr. Kha breaks into a high-pitched giggle. Slowly it spreads to the front seat, where it becomes a roar. Cung is pounding the steering wheel. The four Vietnamese are in hysterics.

"What is it?" I demand. "Come on, you guys, what's the big joke?"

"Oh my, this is very amusing," Mr. Kha gasps between giggles. "When Tra made the arrangements, Duy thought—oh my!" He takes out a handkerchief to wipe his glasses. "We have a famous general with the same name as Tra. Duy thought he was getting—*oh my!*"

We certainly were a great comedown. General Tran Van Tra, an old Viet Minh warrior, had been one of the NVA's chief commanders, leading the attack on Saigon during Tet '68 and helping to direct the final offensive in 1975. In 1982 he published a colorful account of the war that was peppered with criticism of the leadership in Hanoi and was quickly withdrawn from circulation.

With Duy in the car we were in the hands of a genuine operator, tireless, efficient, and transparently condescending. He chatted in French with Maggie like an old aristocrat (which I believe he was), he instructed young Tra in the art of finessing American tourists (addressing him as "General" long after the joke had worn thin), and he fibbed outrageously to embellish a fact or improve a story. Since I scarcely bothered to hide my disbelief, I found myself on the receiving end of his sharpest digs. I didn't ask what he did during the war; he didn't offer to tell me, either. Duy was one complex fellow. Quang Tri Tourism may have been his official job, but he let us know that he had other, unspecified irons in the fire.

Route 9 runs west and south from Dong Ha, ascending through hill country to the Laotian border by a network of bridges. The reason we're traveling Route 9 this morning is that it meanders past the ghosts of Camp Carroll, Khe Sanh, Lang Vei, and other sad ephemera of the American presence. I'm learning about Route 9 from the ground up, so to speak, and I'm trying to get my bearings. For one thing, I see trees, vines, and forest, but I don't see jungle. Slowly I adjust to the fact that I will never see jungle on this trip through Vietnam, but not because of the effects of past defoliation or the present ravages of illegal logging. "Jungle" is a semantic concept that no longer exists, at least not if I wish to be ecologically correct. Dense tropical vegetation in its primeval state is now called rain forest, as in "Save the Amazonian Rain Forest" (by eating your pint of Ben & Jerry's ice cream). "Rain forest" is not only a more accurate designation, it is free of the old

Rudyard Kipling taint of the white man's burden. "Jungle" implies sneaky menace and primitive violence, a useful concept during the war, when American kids from Kansas and Nebraska were trained as "jungle fighters" to extirpate the devious Communist enemy. What would happen if you called a man a rain-forest fighter? I think you'd knock some of the macho wind out of his sails.

Vietnam has a big deforestation problem. We were wicked culprits during our war, when our bombs, napalm, and defoliants destroyed about 14 percent of South Vietnam's forests, but many factors, poignant and ineluctable, contribute to the present crisis. Since the beginning of World War II, Vietnamese forest land, north and south, has shrunk by half from the combined assaults of war, human encroachment and settlement, postwar building and reconstruction, uncontrolled and illegal logging for export, domestic firewood consumption (firewood is still the chief source of cooking and heating fuel for the majority of the population, and the fuel source as well for brickmaking and tea and tobacco processing), slash-and-burn farming by ethnic hill people, and the usual accidental destruction caused by pests and wildfires. Remaining forest land currently hovers at twenty-three million acres, or one-quarter of the land mass, according to the United Nations Development Program, but only five million acres are prime and pristine. By comparison, forest still covers about two-thirds of Cambodia.

With the loss of forests comes the loss of an entire fragile ecosystem—tropical birds, vanishing primates, and rare mammal species whose existence may be unknown to the Western world. In 1993 an elusive cowlike goat, or goatlike cow, with the long horns of an antelope, was discovered by scientists in a protected forest southwest of Hanoi. The forest goat, as local peasants called it, was the first new mammal to be identified by Western zoologists in fifty years. It was officially named a Pseudoryx and written up in *Nature,* the esteemed British journal.

A cash-starved economy like Vietnam's is easy prey to foreign timber interests. How can a poor country be expected to find the moral wherewithal to resist the short-term profits? The pressures come from Thailand, which depleted its own hardwood forest reserves in record time, and from Japan, which had little in the way of forest to begin with. Vietnamese teak and mahogany ends up in those countries, manufactured into furniture and parquet floors; other hardwoods end life ignominiously as high-grade plywood. Pleiku, in the central highlands, is the red-hot hub of the logging trade. Indeed, the economy of the central highlands is driven by felled logs. A case could be made that it was enterprising of local officials, after the devastation Pleiku suffered during the war, to build up a profitable timber industry and create employment in sawmills, if the loss of irreplaceable natural resources weren't so drastic. Because the raw timber is shipped out of the country (from the ports of Qui Nhon and Saigon), the larger profits that accrue in manufacturing and selling the finished products are lost as well. Lost in transit, so to speak. Manufacturing, of course, requires an infusion of capital and up-to-date technology, two things in shorter supply in Vietnam at the present moment than trees in the forest, thanks to twenty years of economic isolation.

As it happens, Vietnam is not without an articulate home-grown environmental protection movement, nor is it without a vocal group of international environmental watchdogs who rage about the ongoing destruction. The Hanoi government has all the protective legislation it needs, on paper, against

nonselective logging and raw timber exports, but enforce-
ment in the provinces is negligible. Reforestation efforts thus
far have failed to keep up with the annual depletion.

"This is the old French road," says Duy as we drive on a
stretch of crumbling blacktop.

"And now we are on the American road," Tra remarks
moments later. The American road, I can't help but notice, is
cement-surfaced and wider.

"So which road do you like better, guys?" Tra smirks, but
he doesn't answer. He is used to my impertinences by now,
but he doesn't like to give me my satisfaction. *I—can't get—
no—sa-tis-faction. Well, I try— There will be an answer, let it
beeee.* Vietnam-era songs are popping into my brain.

"The point," grumbles Mr. Kha, "is that nobody is repair-
ing the roads. This is disgraceful."

"We are crossing the bridge the Americans built."

"I see."

"To your left is the bridge the Americans destroyed."

I crane my neck at two hulks of dazzling white concrete
that sprawl in the river, twin halves of a span, their rusty
steel rebar twisting like broken clock springs. "I see."

What I see is madness.

French engineers started paving Route 9 and bridging the
rivers in 1904 to open the region for their colonial plantations, taking advantage of a well-traveled trading route
through the Truong Son Mountains, or the Annamite chain,
as it was known in those years. Since the French had colo-
nized neighboring Laos as well, their road crews didn't need
to stop at the Viet-Lao border. Route 9 traversed the narrow
Laotian panhandle to the Lao market town of Savannakhet
on the border of Thailand, as it still does. Route 9 and its
bridges saw some heavy fighting in the first Indochina war.

For our war, the Seabees laid new steel plates and fresh concrete on the seasonally flooded, washed-out parts of the
Vietnamese section. French bridges and culverts that were
casualties of the first war were replaced by American bridges
and culverts that suffered a similar fate a few years later.
Build it, blow it—the story of war. Route 9 is taking us
through some beautiful country. Steep cliffs, thick forests,
rushing streams, emerald green valleys. If it weren't for the
occasional wrecked bridge, it would be hard to reconcile this
landscape with warfare. Maybe it was all a bad dream.
Maybe it never happened.

"Camp Carroll," says Duy.

"This is it?"

"This is it. A state pepper plantation."

We get out of the car to look at the shrubby vines trained
to lean and twine on the trunks of jackfruit trees. Built for
the marines in 1966, manned by army artillery units during
the siege of Khe Sanh, Camp Carroll had been turned over
to the ARVNs under Vietnamization. But not for long. During the Eastertide offensive, an ARVN colonel surrendered
the base intact to the North Vietnamese Army. I put on my
glasses to read a stone marker. It commemorates "the surrender of the Saigon puppet to the Army of Liberation."

A few minutes later we draw up to a rocky peak with an
unnaturally flattened top.

"The Rockpile," Duy announces.

In the summer of 1966 a marine reconnaissance team
selected this seven-hundred-foot summit as an observation
post between Khe Sanh and Camp Carroll. A battery of 175-
mm long-range artillery pieces was helicoptered in to the top
of the peak to provide covering fire during operations. The
Rockpile was abandoned when Khe Sanh was abandoned. So
much for the Rockpile.

There are other legendary hills around here that Duy identifies for us by their numbers, which refer to their height in
meters, the standard identification system in warfare. Hill
881 North. Hill 881 South. Hill 861. Hill 950. Hill 1015. A
lot of lives on both sides were lost on these numbered hills
before and during the siege of Khe Sanh. The scarified peaks
are pocked with clumps of vegetation, but the red clay terrain
between them is still fairly barren. The ordnance dropped on
the Khe Sanh region every day during 1967 and 1968, I've
read, was triple the daily tonnage dropped in the European
theater during World War II. I would like to believe that is
an exaggeration. After the war, I've read, five thousand Vietnamese lost their lives here attempting to clear the cratered
landscape of undetonated shells. I would like to believe that
is an exaggeration. The terrain I see is picked clean of ordnance and empty of population. It isn't pretty. It's a stretch of
scrubby, uninhabited badlands with some pockmarked hills.

"No more hills, please," I say. "Let's just go to Khe Sanh."

"And now we are crossing the Cuban bridge."

"The Cuban bridge?"

"Built after the war," Tra tells me.

"Really!"

The French adventurers who came to Khe Sanh in the
1920s to try their luck as planters said the rolling green hills
and red clay soil reminded them of Tuscany. Upon closer
examination, the appropriated land that would make their
fortunes was a triple-canopy rain forest inhabited by elephants, snakes, gibbons, monkeys, and tigers. Even the
greenswards that looked so inviting were not what they
seemed; they were savannas of elephant grass, coarse, man-
high blades that ripped your clothes and nicked the skin like
razors. And the indigenous human population in the Khe

Sanh hills, to whom the land theoretically belonged, weren't really Vietnamese. They were shorter, stockier, stronger-featured, and spoke their own Mon-Khmer language. The hill people hunted with crossbows on ancestral lands that extended into neighboring Laos. They rotated their crops on slash-and-burn cycles and worshiped implacable spirits in trees and rocks. Lowland Vietnamese called them Moi, or "savage." French ethnographers called them the Bru. The planters found them to be honest, industrious workers.

Khe Sanh was too chilly and damp for rubber, but coffee trees suited the foggy hills. Eugene Poilane, the original white settler, was the stuff of colonial legend, an amateur botanist who spawned Eurasian progeny with fecund abandon. Rather than go home to France, his divorced wife set up her own coffee plantation. In time an entire expatriate community was exporting coffee from the Khe Sanh hills, shipping the beans via Route 9 to the Savannakhet market. Felix Poilane, of the second generation, got two harvests a year for an annual cash crop of $250,000 in 1960 dollars.

Khe Sanh town, where the colonials had their villas, was rife with intrigue. Over a thirty-year period a planter had to contend, in overlapping sequence, with the Japanese, the Viet Minh, the Viet Cong, the South Vietnamese, the North Vietnamese, and the American presence. A similar confluence of conflicting ideologies and purposes impacted on the local Bru, whose animist beliefs, physical ailments, and malarial woes attracted the attention of Christian missionaries who arrived bearing medical kits and offers of spiritual salvation. As a matter of historical record, six months before the first Green Berets set foot in the valley, John and Carolyn Miller, a fundamentalist team from the Wycliffe Bible Translators of California, opened a mission up the road from Khe Sanh to put the New Testament in the Bru language.

A mere seven miles from the Laotian border, Khe Sanh Combat Base just growed like Topsy, a perfect microcosm of the Vietnam War. During the Kennedy era, the Green Berets set up a small Special Forces camp on a plateau near Felix Poilane's plantation to instruct the Bru in counterinsurgency strikes, replacing their crossbows with M-1 rifles. Under Lyndon Johnson, General Westmoreland widened the airstrip and sent in a marine battalion. When the marines moved in, Special Forces moved out, to set up a new camp and listening post up the road at Lang Vei, two miles from the border. The Khe Sanh bunkers that had housed the Berets ballooned into a massive garrison of six thousand men defended by planes, bombs, and heavy artillery on the surrounding hills.

Laos was the point of it all, from the American perspective. The Lang Vei trainees were supposed to fight a rearguard action against the Laotian Communist insurgents, the Pathet Lao. Khe Sanh Combat Base was to be the jumping-off place for a full-scale invasion of Laos, a final and complete interdiction of the Ho Chi Minh Trail, a wider war. It's less clear what the North Vietnamese had in mind for Khe Sanh, but the upshot was a costly strategy that seems to have been abandoned. On the other hand, it can also be viewed as a brilliant feint before Tet. Using pack bikes, elephants, and the usual foot power, two NVA divisions had come down the trail through Laos in late 1967, their movements picked up by ultrasonic sensors. Reinforcing the base camp, Westmoreland awaited a set-piece confrontation. LBJ had a mock-up of the camp in his basement situation room: "I don't want any damned Din Bin Phoo."

For eleven weeks between January and March 1968, the marines of Khe Sanh were trapped by North Vietnamese artillery fire. Route 9 was cut. Daily airlifts from Danang resupplied the base camp. When it got too dangerous for cargo planes to land on the strip, the air force resorted to parachute drops. Up at Lang Vei, the Special Forces camp was overrun and abandoned. Somehow, despite all the sophisticated aerial surveillance, radio intercepts, electronic sensors, smoke detectors, urine sniffers, and other gee-whiz technology our side employed to monitor the Ho Chi Minh Trail, the North Vietnamese had managed to slip in a number of tanks. Tanks! They had tanks! Staggering into Khe Sanh, the Lang Vei survivors said some of the tanks had been driven by women. Like a maddened Zeus hurling thunderbolts from the sky, General Westmoreland ordered B-52s and fighter-bombers from bases as far away as Guam and Thailand to commence Operation Niagara, converging in the airspace to drop a hundred thousand tons of bombs on the Khe Sanh valley. Then the NVA vanished. After enough time had elapsed so it didn't look like cause and effect, the marines vanished too.

March 1968, while Khe Sanh was still "holding," was the single most cataclysmic month in the single most cataclysmic year in modern American history. The political pundits who'd crowed that the VC were finished were still trying to explain the Tet Offensive. Khe Sanh's embattled, besieged marines were the subject of a grim cover story in *Newsweek* and back-to-back reports on the Cronkite evening news. Asked for a new estimate of how the war was going and what it would take to win, General Westmoreland called for another 206,000 troops. Elsewhere in Vietnam, another grim event took place that March, although news of the bloody massacre we know as My Lai was concealed from the American public for another year and a half.

Campaigning in the New Hampshire primary that March on just one issue, an end to the war, a little-known senator from Minnesota, Eugene McCarthy, won 45 percent of the vote and came close to beating President Johnson—a feat he accomplished on practically no money, aided by a legion of college kids and the actor Paul Newman. Within days, a wavering Senator Robert F. Kennedy entered the race. Confronted with two Democratic candidates opposed to his war, LBJ gave a nationally televised address to the nation, ostensibly to announce another halt in the bombing of Hanoi and Haiphong. The shocker came in the closing minutes of the president's speech, when he said he would not seek reelection.

As event piled on event in the next few months, the seismic waves ripped through a polarized nation. Martin Luther King, an outspoken opponent of the war, was assassinated in Memphis that April; the black ghettos exploded in rage. The same month, a student uprising led by the militant leftists of SDS closed down Columbia University; blacks and whites occupied separate buildings. Robert Kennedy was assassinated in June, minutes after his victory in the bitter primary in California.

Khe Sanh Combat Base was abandoned in early July, its metal airstrip rolled up, its bunkers exploded. News of the withdrawal was leaked by a reporter; the American command had tried to impose a blanket of silence. General Westmoreland, who'd staked his military reputation and his strategy for Vietnam on such increasingly hollow concepts as "war of attrition," "body counts," and "holding" Khe Sanh—and who was caught by surprise by the Tet Offensive—was replaced in Saigon that month by Creighton Abrams. For the dug-in marines, who'd been commanded to hold their base, and who had done so convinced they were performing a necessary, heroic action, it was an ignominious departure: the army's First Cavalry was sent in to reopen Route 9 and relieve them.

About the only thing either side accomplished during the

terrible siege had been death and destruction. More than ten thousand North Vietnamese soldiers lost their lives at Khe Sanh, blown to bits in their hastily dug trenches and tunnels. American deaths probably exceeded one thousand. Countless civilians, mostly Bru, were felled by the bombs and artillery fire. Countless, that is, because no one was counting. Returning to check on his coffee trees after the siege, Felix Poilane was killed when his plane crash-landed; his wife left for France. John and Carolyn Miller, the missionary couple, resettled at Ban Me Thuot, where they were captured and expelled from Vietnam in 1975 when the Communists took over. Their Bru New Testament was completed six years later back in the States.

"Spooky, unbearably spooky, spooky beyond belief," Michael Herr wrote in *Dispatches* of Khe Sanh plateau.

Khe Sanh, as Maggie and I approach it, is still unbearably spooky, a barren moonscape of rutted red clay, the ghostly outlines of the abandoned airstrip visible under a leaden sky. We walk with timidity, we two American women, letting Duy be our point man on this eerie occasion.

"Mr. Duy, is it safe?" asks Maggie.

"Of course," he answers, skipping ahead, leaping over pot-holes, avoiding the mud. There's nothing to do but follow. Mr. Kha and Tra bring up the rear.

I am the eternal doubter. "Mr. Duy, I want to make sure. This is Khe Sanh Combat Base?" It's so empty, so completely empty. What did I expect to find? Mud-caked marines doing the Khe Sanh Shuffle, the Vietnam version of duck and cover? A discarded can of C-rations? They hated the salty ham and limas, they loved the peaches. A universal truth of the Vietnam War. We walk down the runway to a big stone marker. Most of the lettering is in Vietnamese, but smack in the middle I read, THIS AREA OF TACON PONT BASE BUILT BY U.S. AND SAIGON PUPPET. And lower down, in quotation marks, "Another Dien Bien Phu."

"Tacon Pont? What's that?"

"The name of the village."

"Point," offers Mr. Kha. "They may have meant 'point.' The people who made the sign weren't writing in their own language."

"No, I guess they weren't." Ta Con, or Ta Cong, as the Americans spelled it, had been a Bru village before it was swallowed up by the American base.

"Nothing will grow here," Duy intones. "We don't know what chemicals the Americans poured on the ground."

"On the airstrip? Why would they have poured chemicals on the airstrip?" My voice is testy. The chronology of Khe Sanh Combat Base didn't end with the 1968 siege and evacuation. In 1971 U.S. Army engineers rebuilt the bridges and culverts along Route 9 and replated Khe Sanh's airstrip to help the ARVNs with their ill-fated Laos invasion, an operation that went by the names of Lam Son 719 and Dewey Canyon II. By 1973 Khe Sanh had become an NVA base and airfield, and a site for Soviet-made surface-to-air missiles. These grid marks ossified in red clay may or may not be an American ghost.

"It looks to me," I venture, "like the earth is compacted from metal plates."

"I tell you, they poured chemicals."

"I'm saying that the earth looks compacted from the weight of aircraft. Heavy aircraft bouncing on a metal grid."

We break off the stupid quibble when Tra walks over. "What is the name for this in English?" he asks, extending his hand.

"Barbed wire." I spit out the words because I'm so angry at

Duy. Tra spells them carefully into his book. "Tra, here's another one. Concertina wire. It came in rolls."

Maggie has moved to the other end of the field. She is stalking three gaunt youths in tattered clothes, patched remnants of old army shirts and pants. One has a rifle. The other two are carrying long, thin rods. They are scrap metal hunters, probing the red clay for slender gleanings. No, they can't be. *It's been twenty-five years.* They must be a mirage, an illusion.

"Mr. Duy?" Maggie coos in honeyed tones that mean business. "These very interesting young men don't want me to take their picture."

The youths unleash a torrent of Vietnamese.

"They want a dollar. Then you can take their picture."

"Mr. Duy, please explain to them that it's unethical for a professional photographer to pay for a picture."

The surly dowsers are unimpressed by American ethics. No dollar, no picture. To break the standoff, one of them digs into his pants pocket and pulls out a chain of dog tags. He shoves them into the photographer's hands. They are lousy imitations. Impressions of impressions. Maggie is rooted to the spot, uncertain, fingering the cheap tin, reading the names, the ranks, the religious preferences.

"Don't fall for it, Maggie," I say in disgust. "The dog tags are fake."

Duy cuts me off. "I absolutely guarantee the dog tags are genuine."

"Baloney," I shout. "There's an industry in phony dog tags. You think I don't know that?" I stomp toward the car. It's chilly; I need my down vest. Well, the marines always said it was cold at Khe Sanh. They weren't fooling. Collecting myself, I rummage through my suitcase. In a second I find what I want—a plastic key-chain flashlight that lights when you squeeze it.

"Here," I say to the most belligerent dowser. "Made in America." For all I know, he'll spit in my face.

With as much of a smile as this sad youth can muster, he takes the flashlight and strings it onto the amulet chain around his neck. Gravely he nods. We've reached an accord. Now Maggie can take her pictures.

"Hah!" Duy scoffs. "Good till the battery runs out, then you throw it away."

Back in the car, Maggie and I have run out of songs. We've been singing dopey duets ever since we arrived in Khe Sanh valley. A tisket, a tasket. Blue Moon. No pattern. Whatever pops into her head or mine, as long as it lightens our mood. Maggie, God bless her, can carry a tune. I was one of those kids the music teacher put in the back row and called "a listener." If our serenading is having any effect on our companions, they're going to remarkable lengths not to show it. They burrow into a stubborn funk whenever Maggie tries to tease them into a reciprocal number.

"Mr. Duy?" she implores in her lilting cadence. "I'll bet you know some wonderful songs."

Silence.

"Mr. Kha? You're holding out on us, Mr. Kha."

"Okay," I announce. "I've got one. I am now going to sing an American antiwar song. Country Joe and the Fish. Woodstock, 1969."

> *Well, it's one, two, three, what are we fighting for?*
> *Don't ask me, I don't give a damn. Next stop is Viet-Nam.*
> *And it's five, six, seven, open up the pearly gates—*

I break off abruptly. I can't remember the next line. Something about dying, coming home in a box. Maybe this wasn't such a hot idea. The silence from the Vietnamese is deafening.

"It's an antiwar song," I repeat lamely.

There's a brief powwow in the front seat, and then, at Duy's cue, the men begin singing in Vietnamese. Tra's baritone throbs with militant passion. Cung's beautiful tenor floats through the car. Even Mr. Kha is spirited and on key.

> *Soldiers of Vietnam, we go forward,*
> *Struggling for the people's cause.*
> *Marching to the field of battle,*
> *Forward!*
> *Our Vietnam is eternal, strong.*

When they finish the anthem they lapse back into silence. A glummer funk than before. Duy starts them up again. This time I can tell it's a love song.

"Lunch today is in Khe Sanh town. If time permits, explore the ruins of this lovely old French colonial *ville*. This afternoon we follow a winding path through the mountains and ford a stream to a Bru Van Kieu village." I'm composing an imaginary tourist brochure. Lunch today is inedible. It doesn't help that a dog has urinated near our table and nobody is bothering to wipe up the puddle. At least there's beer for the three men who aren't driving. Cung and Maggie and I are sticking to Coke.

Four men and a woman are the only other customers in the place. A loud party, hard, young, and blotto. Out of boredom they're building a wobbly pyramid of empty beer cans on the floor. One of them chugalugs and chucks the empty onto the pile.

"Not good people," says Tra. "Smugglers from Laos."

"Laotian smugglers?"

"Vietnamese smugglers," Duy says with impatience.

I keep forgetting how close we are to the border. I also keep forgetting how the long arm of the United States prevented countries like Thailand and Japan from doing business with Vietnam until a few years ago, and how hungry the Vietnamese are for consumer goods. The smugglers buy Thai-manufactured clothes and Japanese electronics in Savannakhet and bring them in via Route 9. That's how the Seiko watches got to the Dong Ha market, and it probably explains my imported Coke. The other big smuggling route comes down from the north. The Chinese are dumping cheap manufactured goods into Vietnam, mostly textiles, shoes, bicycles, and cigarettes, undercutting local prices and exacerbating their strained relations with Hanoi. For now the two illegal trade routes are greased by a lot of bribes. If Vietnam's privatization continues and its trade relations are normalized in a true market economy, the smugglers will become ordinary business people, contending with the more usual risks of international competition.

I pick up the check, which comes to eight dollars, and then we buy some bags of hard candy to bring to the Bru. Maggie says she has more than enough medicine in her emergency kit.

The road to the Bru Van Kieu village of Lang Cat is indeed winding and beautiful. Either I'm witnessing the miraculous regenerative powers of tropical vegetation, or this particular stretch somehow escaped the destruction. From the car window we get an occasional glimpse of someone who is unmistakably "ethnic," tall, proud, wrapped in a woven sarong with a cloth headdress, carrying bundles of firewood. I'd like to stop and say hello, and Maggie is itching to take pictures, but Duy is firm about driving on. These tribespeople aren't Bru; they're from another minority, one that is not amenable to strangers with cameras. Duy is responsible for our safety, and the gentle Bru of Lang Cat are used to being ogled. That's what unnerves me. I'd rather get rebuffed in a spontaneous encounter than be led by the nose through a showcase village.

Cung stays with the car while Duy leads us, Indian file, down a narrow trail. After a ten-minute trek, we reach a gurgling brook strewn with boulders. Lang Cat is on the opposite bank. Already we've attracted some village children who are whooping and pointing, as children do. Nimbly the guides hop from rock to stone, ferrying Maggie's equipment to the other side. Their shoes, I notice, are perfectly dry. Next, the surefooted photographer makes it across. "Wait for me," I wail. Removing my sneakers and socks, I wade between the slippery boulders, lurching on pebbles, drenching my rolled-up khakis, a figure of rare hilarity to the children.

In retrospect I needn't have been so morbidly self-conscious about ogling the Bru, since one obvious tradeoff is that the Bru get to ogle the silly tourists. About fifty villagers, young and old, male and female, gather to watch us admire their longhouses, their wood mortars and pestles, their pigs and their chickens.

"Give out the candy!" Duy scolds.

Give out the candy? I balk, shrinking at the Lady Bountiful role. Impatiently Duy takes the bag and distributes small handfuls. Here a little, there a little. He does it with real panache, enjoying himself. For their part, the Bru take the offerings with sweet, noncommittal smiles. No one pushes for more, and no one refuses him, either. If there's one intrusion the Bru are inured to, it's the Vietnamese civil servant.

Sartorially, the Bru are in transition, with the women favoring machine-made shirts and wraparound sarongs. The old women blacken their teeth and cover their heads, the younger ones prefer beads and earrings. The men have no special dress.

We are joined on our walk by the village teacher, a painfully introverted young Vietnamese who matriculated at the teachers' college in Hue. His stint at Lang Cat, he says through the guides, is a three-year assignment.

"Assignment? He didn't volunteer?" My American individualism has trouble digesting the concept. The government is doing a good thing by putting trained teachers in these ethnic enclaves, but the young man looks woefully lonely, if not clinically depressed.

"Not so terrible," Mr. Kha consoles. "Next time he'll get a better post."

Dutifully we climb a ladder into a thatched longhouse built on log stilts. Stilted longhouses are a protection against flooding; the Bru keep their livestock penned down below. As many Bru as can fit climb in after us with a restless air of expectation. In one regard I feel right at home. Male and female, the Bru are serious smokers who grow a fine crop of their own tobacco. Lighting up with the crowd, I hand around a pack of Carltons. The younger men are eager to try one; the older women stick to their long-stemmed pipes. I lean back and relax. It's pleasantly somnambulistic to sit cross-legged in the smoke-filled longhouse, puffing away, ogling and ogled by fifty Bru. Cinema verité. An afternoon at the movies. The little things are what I'm after. The teacher, I notice, has a special friend, a male companion. Good. So he's not totally isolated after all.

"Ask them questions!" Duy prods.

Oh, that again—the forced performance. What a killjoy,

that Duy. Picking out a grizzled old man with a wonderful face, I reluctantly ask what he did during the war.

The response comes back: "I stayed here and farmed." Considering the company, it's a politic answer. The Bru, intent on survival, worked both sides of the fence, just like the French planters, just like many Vietnamese. For the life of me, I can't think of another question.

At a loss for what to do next, I pull a purple Space Tube out of my bag. At home I keep one of these magic wands with its floating potpourri of stars and crescents on my coffee table. Something to play with and stare at when guests come over. It seemed like a neat idea to bring one to Vietnam as a symbol showing that American technology can be whimsical and benign. Now that I'm sitting in Lang Cat, my gift no longer seems clever, but it's all I've got.

"For the teacher," I say, passing the wand.

At first he's perplexed by the Lucite tube, then he catches on. He passes it to his friend, who tips and turns it, making the glittery particles rise and fall.

Duy is watching intently. "One present?" he scowls. "You brought one present for four hundred people?"

Maggie has opened her medical kit, courtesy of an earlier assignment for *National Geographic*. "This is for coughs," she says to the teacher via the guides. "This is for skin rash." He nods uncertainly, worried he'll forget or get it wrong. "This is for headaches."

I'm admiring Maggie's grace under pressure when someone pokes me through a slat in the longhouse. Down below, a woman is appealing mutely. There's a nasty tumor over her eye. She is joined by another woman, who points to her throat. Beyond these two a line is forming. Maggie and I exchange helpless glances. The medical needs of Lang Cat are beyond two scouts from a travel magazine.

"I think we should leave," I tell Duy.

"What?" he snaps. "You've seen only one longhouse."

"There's nothing we can do for them. We want to leave *now*."

Tra speaks up. "They've had enough," he says sharply.

The Bru accept our departure by losing interest. I can't say I blame them. We aren't a very rewarding spectacle after all.

The forces behind the newly opened Truong Son Hotel, Dong Ha's grandest, must have given up on the concept of guests at a critical moment in its construction. I sat on the bed in my room and tried to figure out what had happened. The ceiling joints were so badly fitted that patches of sky peeped through at the corners. Industrial-sized electrical transformers, sockets that sprouted exposed wires, and giant switch plates that turned nothing on or off had been punched into the walls in profusion. A smeary coat of blue paint, so thin that it covered nothing, had been hastily applied to the plasterboard. Topping off the decor, a limp piece of cloth that passed for a curtain hung askew on the window.

Okay, so maybe the "foreign experts," perhaps a team of Russians, had been called home in mid-project. Okay, so somebody had delivered the wrong electrical equipment and the poor blokes who'd been assigned to install it didn't have a clue as to what they were doing. Okay, so the prefabricated slabs of plasterboard had been cut poorly at the factory and the local carpenters who'd attempted to fit the joints were rank neophytes at their jobs. But what about the single coat of blue paint? Any idiot can paint a wall. There was only one possible explanation. Somewhere along the line, at the factory, at the construction site, or plausibly at both places, the duly requisitioned cans of paint had been watered down shamelessly so that someone (probably lots of someones) could make off with the good stuff, either for private purposes or to resell it at a pure profit. I was looking at a boondoggle.

Did it matter to anybody in the town of Dong Ha that its premier hotel, so impressive on the outside, was such a disaster inside? Probably not. We were, I think, the only guests.

Duy chose the restaurant and did the ordering amid cheerful greetings from the family of owners. By this time in our travels it was no surprise to Maggie or me that Dong Ha's finest eatery looked like a roadside diner. It *was* a roadside diner, catering to truckers on the smuggling route. Illegally imported jackets and pants hung on the walls, giving the place a boutique effect.

Tra excused himself to make a purchase. He came back to the table with a boxed layette set for his infant son and an iridescent zippered jacket for himself. "Last month nineteen dollars, this month twenty-six dollars," he sighed. "Inflation."

"Then why did you buy?"

His eyes widened at my obtuseness. "To have an American bomber jacket, like your men wear at home."

"Like our men wear?" I examined the cardboard tag. It read, "American Bomber Jacket, Made in Thailand."

"Wear it in good health," I said. "An American expression."

The food was a feast, platter after platter, with a tray of crunchy fried songbirds arranged in a circle as the *pièce de résistance*. Maggie dug in; I passed up the fledglings. The beer was flowing freely. Halfway through the meal everyone was tipsy except for Cung and me.

"I do not let Cung drink. Cung has to drive," Tra declared with a comradely hug.

"Cheers," I said to Cung. "You and I stick to Coke. Hey, Cung, you want to see my New York State driver's license?"

Four Vietnamese heads bent over the small rectangle.

"Miss Maggie, Miss Susan. Do you know the Vietnamese saying, what is the definition of paradise?"

"No, Mr. Duy. What is the Vietnamese definition of paradise?"

"Paradise is living in a French house, having a Japanese wife, and eating Chinese food."

"That is very good, Mr. Duy. Paradise is ... I'm writing that down."

"Maggie, Susan, do you know why, when the Vietnamese eat a banana, first they break it in half?"

"No, Mr. Kha, why do the Vietnamese break a banana in half?"

"Because it is, ah—more polite."

"More polite?"

"It is not so ... "

"So *what*, Mr. Kha? I'm getting the idea from your gesture. So phallic?"

"Oh my!"

"Mr. Duy, do you have a card?"

"No, but I have a bicycle."

"She said *card*, Duy, not car! She was asking for your business card."

"Oh my! That is very funny. Do you have a card? No, but I have a bicycle!"

After a while they stopped speaking in English. I looked around the restaurant. A dozen young women, all tarted up in makeup and sharp clothes, were sharing a long table. Huh? Beaming a sisterly smile in their direction, I got back a cool, disinterested flicker. A bell went off in my mind.

Abruptly a fight erupted at our table. Duy was shouting at Mr. Kha. Mr. Kha was matching him decibel for decibel. It sounded mean and angry.

"Stop it, stop it, you two! What's the matter?"

"He accused me of living under two systems!" said Duy.

"I did not!"

"Mr. Duy, please! He did not! Why would Mr. Kha have said that? Mr. Kha meant—he meant that you were very lucky to have *known* two systems. The French and the Americans, and now . . . "

I can't believe I sailed in like that, playing Little Miss Know-Nothing Peacemaker to settle an argument in Vietnamese, but sail in I did. I can't bear shouting. In any event, my ludicrous intervention had a calming effect, and all was forgiven. Maybe. In retrospect I think that Mr. Kha did say to Mr. Duy that he was living under two systems. In retrospect I think the entire town of Dong Ha was living under two systems.

Duy had hinted when we met him that he had a "sideline profession," another job besides Quang Tri Tourism. When we said goodbye to him the day after his fight with Mr. Kha, he mentioned something about how sorry he was that we didn't have time to visit the cemetery. I assumed he meant Truong Son National Cemetery north of Dong Ha, the famous graveyard for soldiers killed on the Ho Chi Minh Trail. Five months later the *Far Eastern Economic Review* carried a report about a scandal at another, newer military cemetery at Dong Ha, where more remains from Vietnam's historic conflicts were to be reinterred. Government investigators had found empty graves, coffins stuffed with animal bones. There was a full-dress trial, resulting in a couple of death sentences. It seems that some Quang Tri province officials, fifty or so people including a police chief and an administrator at Dong Ha's social welfare bureau, had pocketed public funds earmarked for burying the dead. I hope the new cemetery wasn't Duy's "sideline."

It was time to leave the restaurant and go back to the hotel. Wobbly on his feet, Duy whispered in French to Maggie, a classic "The night is young, what a pity to waste it." With gracious aplomb the photographer demurred. As we threaded our way past their table, the young women swiveled in their chairs to give Maggie and me a practiced appraisal, checking our clothes. Unimpressed, they went back to their food.

"Tomorrow at seven-thirty," Duy said in the lobby. "I take you to a good place for morning *pho*."

"Mr. Duy," I said, "I'm not thinking about breakfast. That table of women in the restaurant, what do they do for a living?"

"What women?"

"The long table of twelve women wearing full makeup and dressy clothes. How do they earn their living?"

"Ah, the women!" he said, nearly falling over. "Why, they are kitchen workers!"

In the morning I went downstairs to the hotel dining room in search of a cup of coffee. Armed with mops and pails, the maintenance staff appeared to be holding a meeting in the banquet hall. I peeked through the double doors. They were watching a kung fu movie on a video screen.

My presence in the empty dining room startled the young waitress, who flew over to replace the spotted, stained tablecloth with a damp cloth that was equally stained. Rushing off again, she returned and timidly plunked down that prize amenity of Asian dining, a toothpick holder. Eventually I got my coffee, French bread, and cheese omelet. It wasn't half bad. Maggie wandered in and ordered the same, savoring the sweetened condensed cream in her coffee. I yearned for regular cow's milk and a snappy American waitress to materialize with a refill. Okay, so I'm not a perfect world traveler.

The guides took a separate table when they saw us, and received their automatic guide fare of packaged instant noodle soup.

We took our bags down to the lobby to wait for Duy. He was disappointed to hear that we'd already had breakfast.

"But I said—"

"We thought it best, Mr. Duy, to get on the road. We're eager to see the Vinh Moc tunnels."

Cung brought the car around. It had been washed clean of its Khe Sanh mud.

Heading north again on Highway 1.

"And here," says Duy as we pull to a halt, "you may view the McNamara Fence."

"What are you pointing at, Mr. Duy? I don't see a thing. There's nothing there."

The guides start to giggle. I can't help it. I start giggling too.

If one hotel boondoggle in Dong Ha gets my back up, what is the civilized response to the McNamara Fence—a.k.a. McNamara's Wall, a.k.a., in a bow to the Maginot, the McNamara Line—a billion-dollar technological boondoggle, call it what you will, of which not a trace remains?

It was the dream of Robert S. McNamara in 1967 to string a barbed-wire barrier across the DMZ from the South China Sea to Laos, a distance of approximately thirty-five miles, to keep the North Vietnamese Army from crossing the seventeenth parallel by foot. A second barrier would span the Laotian panhandle to the Thai border and plug up the Ho Chi Minh Trail. The fence was to be fortified by electronic sensors monitored by aircraft that would relay the data to a computer center in Thailand, vectoring instant air attacks.

Within the wire thicket, the ground was to be seeded with antipersonnel "gravel" mines composed of explosive plastic pellets. (A plastic pellet does not show up on X-rays, which means that every wound has to be treated by exploratory surgery.) For conventional backup there would be a network of combat bases and reaction-force troops.

A numbers cruncher in his previous job as head of Ford Motor Company, Secretary of Defense McNamara calculated that his high-tech barrier would raise the cost per foot soldier so steeply that the powers in Hanoi would cease their infiltration. The fence would also be a prime deterrent if the North should ever try a "human wave" assault across the DMZ, as in the Korean War, when North Korean troops poured across the thirty-eighth parallel. Supplies were ordered and erection of the fence actually began before the Tet Offensive and the siege of Khe Sanh made it evident that the Vietnamese were conducting their war differently. A physical barrier studded with electronic gadgetry, much of it passing through mountainous terrain, was too naive to be worth completing. For starters, the work crews were easy targets for North Vietnamese artillery fire.

Minutes after breaching the McNamara Fence, we reached the Ben Hai River, the natural barrier at the seventeenth parallel separating the North and the South. It was drizzling again. I got out of the car to stretch my legs while Maggie photographed the ironwork bridge and the monument commemorating a reunited Vietnam. Three American tourists were recording the spot with their cameras.

One turned out to be a veteran, Tim Schuster from Woodstock, New York. Tim said he'd enlisted in the air force in 1967 and signed on for intelligence work. He'd been stationed at Tan Son Nhut airbase, Dalat, and Nha Trang. After his tour he became an antiwar activist, joining the MOBE

(Mobilization to End the War in Vietnam) and going to Washington for the big demonstrations.

Tim still wore his hair long. He had become a permanent counterculture person. "Vietnam turned my life around," he said, stating the obvious. Shaking his head, he lapsed into sixties vernacular. "This trip is blowing my mind. I met a guy in Hanoi at a bar, and we figured out that he was being born under a kitchen table while people I knew were bombing his city. Death and life, the cycle goes on."

Our destination was on the other side of the Ben Hai River, a coastal village called Vinh Moc, home of what was reputedly the best defensive tunnel system in North Vietnam.

People have different responses when they try to imagine life during wartime. Whenever I put myself inside the nightmare, I don't think of manning a machine gun, capturing a ridge, patrolling a perimeter, or flying a plane. I think about places to hide. Underground shelters have probably been with us since the beginning of warfare, whole populations seeking out the safety of natural caves. As for me, hiding entered my consciousness when I was very young and heard stories of London's bomb shelters during the Blitz, of Jews living secretly in attics and basements, of resistance fighters taking refuge in the sewers of Warsaw and other cities. If war came to Brooklyn, I knew I'd dig a deep hole. A child's terror, but a primeval instinct.

Americans are lucky. We've never been invaded. What do we know about hiding from an enemy who stalks the ground over our heads, who drops bombs on our homes and fields? In truth, what do we know about resistance?

North and South, the Vietnamese resistance dug tunnels and lived underground, attempting to follow three basic precepts: "Walk without footprints, cook without smoke, and speak without sound." Not every tunnel, with its requisite air vent and camouflaged escape hatch, had the advantage of good hard soil and wood-beam reinforcement. Untold numbers of tunnels collapsed, burying the inhabitants alive under cave-ins caused by aboveground tank movements, or by bombs and shells that scored a direct hit or landed close enough to produce fatal tremors. And many were discovered, grenaded, and gassed by American patrols. Small and lithe enough to burrow into narrow passageways without getting stuck, the American demolition experts who specialized in destroying these Viet Cong hideouts called themselves tunnel rats.

Of all the tunnels built by the Vietnamese, Americans are most familiar with Cu Chi, a two-hundred-mile labyrinth north of Saigon, where Viet Cong sappers hid under the nose of the U.S. command. But the buzz on Cu Chi was that it had become a sort of Coney Island amusement attraction, with a Coke machine and a shooting range—your choice of an American M-16 or a Russian AK-47. According to the *Lonely Planet* guidebook, the infrequently visited Vinh Moc tunnels, located just north of the DMZ, were an important way station for supplies on the Ho Chi Minh Trail, and were still the real thing.

Tran Minh Ngoi, the prideful keeper of the tunnels, was out attending a village wedding when we arrived. One of his sons went to retrieve him. When he returned he eyed us noncommittally and took us into an exhibition hall where photographs told the story of Vinh Moc. It had been a pleasant enough village of thatched-roof houses in 1966. It was a bare stretch of nothing in 1967, after the bombs of Rolling Thunder. By then, the entire population of twelve hundred had moved underground, emerging only to tend their crops and do war work.

Vinh Moc was a popular air-raid target because of its strategic location on the coastline. Chinese trawlers filled with arms and ammunition would anchor off nearby Con Co Island in the middle of the night and wait for the villagers, who would ferry small loads to shore in motorized sampans— a three-hour trip one way. The matériel was then shipped south to Viet Cong contacts or moved overland by bicycle to distribution points on the Ho Chi Minh Trail.

When the bombing raids of Rolling Thunder ceased, the villagers of Vinh Moc resumed a semblance of normal life aboveground. In 1972 they returned to the tunnels when Operation Linebacker commenced. In all, some twelve thousand tons of matériel passed through their hands. Life in the tunnels was not without its simple joys. Seventeen babies were born underground. Once, a touring group of singers from Hanoi came to entertain. Late in the war the villagers rigged up a generator and lights, and even got to watch movies.

The more I looked at the photos, the more I wanted to know.

"Who's that, Ngoi?"

The answer came back in translation. "He invented a special earth-moving machine." (Most other tunnels were dug by hand with small spades.)

"Who is she?"

"She performed an act of sabotage against a U.S. boat." (Besides the bombs, the village was under assault by naval shelling.)

Duy was urging us to speed it up and get to the tunnels, but I thought it might be wise if I took a trip to the bathroom first. I was directed outside to the bushes. Prowling in the wet undergrowth while the rain was falling inhibited my bladder; I decided to wait.

Ngoi was wearing shorts and rubber sandals. He put on a red rain jacket and gave us a flashlight apiece. Duy said he'd accompany us to carry Maggie's camera and an oil lantern she'd bought at the Dong Ha market. Tra and Mr. Kha elected to stay aboveground.

After a quick trot along a path, Ngoi ducked inside an entrance and vanished. I peered into the nothingness. Maybe there were steps and maybe there weren't. All I could see was about six inches of rushing water.

"He says it's dry in there after the first set of steps," Duy reported, disappearing into the hole.

"Maggie, I'm going to twist an ankle."

"You won't twist an ankle. I forgot to tell you I'm claustrophobic."

"I'll go first then."

"No, I'll go."

She went. I brought up the rear, slipping and sliding and sloshing, bumping my head on the ceiling, scraping against walls, waving my flashlight into the void.

"Ngoi, Ngoi, slow down! Maggie, Mr. Duy—where are you? Don't leave me behind!"

Ngoi was right. Inside, on the first of three levels, the tunnels were dry, and the ceiling was high enough in most places for me to stand upright. I trained my flashlight on the cave-like alcoves that were used for family dwellings. Sounds echoed strangely. I had no trouble breathing.

The two miles of tunnel had shunts to twelve concealed exits. We scurried behind Ngoi, who darted down more steps and made decisions about passageways, leading us to a fair-sized meeting hall with room enough for forty people packed tight. Beyond another bend lay the well. I reached through a grate to dip my hand in the cool water. Another few steps down, off by itself in sanitary isolation, was the communal latrine.

Her claustrophobia forgotten, Maggie set up a photo shoot, posing Ngoi with the oil lantern in one of the family alcoves, positioning Duy and me so we could beam our flashlights on his face. Ngoi was a good model. Very patient. Enduring. He complained only a little when the heat from the lantern started burning his hand. We had some good laughs.

We exited the tunnels onto an idyllic bluff where a few cattle were grazing. The rain had stopped. Down below was the sea. A quiet sea. No warships, no shelling, no fishing boats on clandestine missions.

"Did you see the centipedes?" Duy asked.

"No, Mr. Duy. I did not see any centipedes."

"I saw them. I did not want to frighten you."

Ngoi invited us to his house to wash up and share a pot of tea. Exhilarated, our shoes soaked, our clothes muddy, we sprawled on his porch, telling Tra and Mr. Kha what they had missed, while Ngoi's family gathered around the roughhewn table.

"Green tea," said Mr. Kha. "An honor."

Maggie pantomimed that she was leaving the oil lantern for the house and received an appreciative smile. Impulsively she pulled a few vials of hand lotion and skin cream from her exhausted medical kit and gave Ngoi's wife a demonstration. Ngoi's wife looked at Ngoi, bemused.

I produced another of my plastic key-chain flashlights, this one in pink, and presented it to one of Ngoi's kids. He squealed and ran off. The family laughed. I don't think I've ever made a child so happy.

"Ngoi asks if you would like to stay for dinner."

"Really, Mr. Kha? Tell him we'd love to."

When Duy returned from his ablutions, he promptly countermanded the plan, claiming it would take too long to prepare the food. After all, we had to return to Hue that evening.

Ngoi's face fell. My face fell. We exchanged a look that said, "We like each other very much. Why are we being pushed around by this tinhorn bureaucrat? Why are we helpless to do what we want?"

Mortified, Maggie and I fished some dong from our wallets.

"Ngoi thanks you," Mr. Kha translated, "on behalf of the People's Committee."

The regret was palpable on both sides when we left Vinh Moc.

Back in the car, Duy said, "I told that guy to put in a visitors' toilet."

"Really, Mr. Duy, shouldn't Quang Tri Tourism put in the toilet?"

"Anyway, now we have time," he exulted, "to have dinner at a wonderful place in Dong Ha."

Maggie and I got the picture. Maggie and I were fuming.

"You mean, Mr. Duy, that you made us refuse dinner with Ngoi and his family, whom we adored, so we could sit in our muddy clothes in a restaurant in Dong Ha? That is *not* what we'll do. We will check back into the Truong Son Hotel, we will change our clothes, we will put on dry shoes, we will drive straight to Hue, and to hell with dinner!"

I lit a cigarette to compose myself. It was the first time I had smoked in the car. Tra coughed and opened the window.

Duy and Mr. Kha conferred in Vietnamese. I heard the word "Metropole." I imagined that Duy was complaining, "Who are these Americans you brought me? Either they're too cheap to buy dinner or they don't have any money," and Mr. Kha was saying, "Well, in Hanoi they stayed at the Metropole."

On the south side of the Ben Hai River, we paid three dollars at the hotel of boondoggles to shower and change clothes. Then we dropped Duy off near his house and gave him his tip. That was when he said, "What a pity that you don't have time to visit our new cemetery."

When we reached Le Loi Boulevard in Hue, Cung drove past Madame Nhu's old establishment to the new hotel.

"Tra, you got us in! What do we have to pay?"

"After dinner you will conduct an interview with the manager."

Our new digs were certainly a step up. Pretty watercolors on the walls, a capacious bathtub that drew its hot water from a tank with a throw switch, a working elevator, and a zingy crowd of French tourists.

The guides were seated with their colleagues when we entered the dining room. After the closeness of the road it was odd to see them in that context. Hired help.

"Tra, it's been an emotional couple of days. I apologize for snapping at Duy, and I'm sorry I smoked in the car."

"That's *awl*right. I quit smoking six months ago."

"Well, enjoy your dinner. What have you got there? Rice and cabbage?"

"We don't get what you eat."

Maggie and I summoned our waitress. "Tell the guides' table to order some special dishes and put it on our bill." When we looked over later, they were diving in.

My interview on command with the hotel manager, with Mr. Kha as interpreter, was in a formal conference room twice the size of the central meeting hall in the Vinh Moc tunnels. Nguyen Phung Hung, deputy director of Hue Tourism and vice director of the Hotel Hue, had news. The hotel, which at fifty dollars a night had already captured the upscale crowd, was about to become a joint venture. For a 50 percent stake in the profits, Hong Kong investors had agreed to upgrade the plumbing, redecorate the 140 rooms, put in a cable TV system, revamp the swimming pool, and resurface the tennis courts.

Punchy with exhaustion, I wished Director Hung and the Hong Kong investors good luck.

The following morning over cheese omelets and French bread (our treat), we said a lingering goodbye to our team, with promises to send language tapes to Tra and clients to Mr. Kha. The gift money, in dollars, had been efficiently portioned by Maggie into white envelopes.

At Phu Bai airport, once a humming American base, Mr. Kha pulled me aside. "If I said something that was critical of the government, you won't write that?"

"Did you say something critical, Mr. Kha? I can't recall. How are you getting back to Hanoi?"

"By train. I have my ticket."

The flight was announced, and we left for Saigon.

SAIGON AND THE DELTA

Saigon. The Continental. I draw back the curtains, throw open the shutters, and step onto the balcony, into the sensory shock of glaring sun and humid air. This is one of those long-anticipated peak moments in travel that invariably reduces me to nervous laughter, when I pinch myself and say aloud, "Hey, babe, you're *here!*"

Map in hand, I look down at the square. Its name is Lam Son, for the village where the fifteenth-century Vietnamese patriot Le Loi was born. Across the way is the Caravelle, where I'm fairly certain Eric Sevareid did his nightly stand-uppers on the roof in 1967, silver hair beneath the low Saigon sky. Strange, the first memory to surface: an American commentator choosing a flattering backdrop for a television war. The building straight ahead reached by the wide stone steps must be the old French opera house, where the National Assembly convened during the Saigon regime. And that narrow street—why, it has to be Dong Khoi, known to American GIs as Tu Do, home of raunchy massage parlors and bawdy dives where B-girls sipped fake champagne called Saigon tea. To the French and to Graham Greene and his readers, Dong Khoi was rue Catinat, street of fine jewelry shops, choice gossip, wild rumors. If I follow Dong Khoi to the river, as Greene and his fictional journalist, Fowler, walked the rue Catinat, I will reach the Majestic, where the price of a drink still includes the best view of Saigon's port.

Some cities intimidate through the memories of writers who've captured the sights and smells with such breathtaking skill that you wonder what's left except to retrace their footsteps. Stand on their rooftops. Drink at the bars they made famous. Pull off a romantic assignation in a sweltering room in a seamy quarter. Wander dark streets in the dead of night giving the high sign for dreamy narcotic pleasure.

I was afraid I was going to fail in Saigon, a rank pretender stumbling in the path of *The Quiet American*. An aging female grown altogether too cautious and weary for the reckless adventures of Marguerite Duras. A passing observer too late by a generation for the brotherhood of foreign correspondents who flocked here and nested, for too many seasons, on the awninged terrace they christened the Continental Shelf.

Outsiders have written extraordinarily well about Saigon, but oddly enough the Vietnamese haven't. The nation's most celebrated poets and writers have come from the northern and central regions.

But fail in Saigon? What a joke. Who didn't fail in Saigon? The French? The Americans? The southern republic, after declaring it the national capital in 1956? Those politically correct, economically disastrous warriors from the North who rolled in amid cheers and cries of liberation in 1975? Even the name they bestowed on their glittering trophy, Ho Chi Minh City, failed to stick. Taking a long view of Saigon's more spectacular failures, one shouldn't forget the Cambodian empire's reversal of fortune; before the Vietnamese continued their advance down the peninsula in the eighteenth century, a Khmer trading port had thrived on the site.

Naturally I was staying at the Continental. I'm a sucker for tradition. From the moment it opened its Belle Epoque doors, the grand hotel had soothed the scalawag international crowd with cool aperitifs, French cuisine, and Viennese waltzes. When André Malraux, chastened by his detention in Phnom Penh for hauling off a cache of Khmer statues, arrived in 1925 to start a newspaper that railed against colonial excess, where else would he and his wife, Clara, rent a room? *L'Indochine*, his reformist paper, lasted nine months, but it wasn't a total loss. The hotel management gave Malraux meals on the house when he couldn't pay his bills.

What had I done to deserve Suite 115? Ah, that was the question. My carpeted two-room extravagance with reproduction Oriental furniture had a giant bed, huge armoires, welcoming bowls of fruit and flowers, a tea set on a carved table, eight lamps, a big tiled bathroom, a mini-fridge and bar stocked with the usual plus (oh joy!) imported Swiss chocolates, a TV and VCR, a complimentary copy of *Vietnam Investment Review*, and the inescapable dented Chinese thermos.

Maggie's suite and terrace were just as grand. From the number of vases filled with fresh flowers, I gathered that word of two scouts for an American travel magazine had reached the front desk.

We all have our connections, however frayed, to Saigon. Mine was film cans and shot lists typed by correspondents who worked for ABC News in the sixties, a sterling team in retrospect—Peter Jennings, Ted Koppel, Tom Jarriel, even for a while Malcolm Browne. In that pre-satellite era, their filmed reports were carried by plane to New York—or to San Francisco, saving three hours—so nothing was exactly same-day current, although it seemed current enough. The hottest stuff was prepared for air by the senior staff. I screened, cut, and fashioned lead-ins and intros for the leftovers that we fed to our affiliates for their 11:00 p.m. shows.

ABC News is a top-notch operation today, but we labored back then at the bottom of the heap as the also-ran network. Cronkite was the news show I watched on my own time. So did everyone else in my shop. CBS was usually the front runner in getting the story, although there were moments when you had to hand it to NBC, like during Tet, when General Loan fired his pistol point-blank into the head of a hand-cuffed Viet Cong suspect on a Saigon street, right in front of the An Quang Pagoda. NBC's cameraman kept rolling while a man's brains exploded and a body in black shorts and a checkered shirt crumpled into a heap.

On the whole, CBS seemed just a little less hawkish than the other two networks, which made CBS appear very brave. Walter Cronkite, that kindly, avuncular figure, had doubts. Well, maybe not doubts, maybe just reservations. Lyndon Baines Johnson thought so. It was public knowledge that LBJ would ring up Frank Stanton, the network president, and scream that Walter and his reporters were sabotaging his war.

My ABC colleagues, an understaffed and grumpy bunch, never dared to question the war. Questioning the war made them very nervous. People in the news business weren't supposed to have opinions—oh, they could have little personal opinions about how the South Vietnamese weren't pulling their oar, something like that, but opinions about what we used to call "our commitment," questions concerning the wisdom and sanity of the president of the United States, were out of bounds. Our quarterbacking sessions, rehashing the Gulf of Tonkin Resolution, reviewing the domino theory, had a way of ending when someone snapped, "I have to believe that my president has information I don't have—I have to believe my government."

Meanwhile, something was happening among the young news clerks and copy assistants. They were letting their hair grow, listening to Bob Dylan, wearing jeans in the office. One day a copy assistant surprised me by laying a packet of pot (he called it grass) on my desk. Another loaned me his paperback of General Giap's *People's War*. Most of the news clerks were college dropouts who had lost their student deferments; they were actively, and somewhat desperately, trying to figure out how to avoid the draft. They had little in common with the writers and producers, who were older and working on their careers.

I was one of two women writers in the news division during those prefeminist times, and my acceptance by my peers was iffy. I was okay on live space shots, those interminable Apollo missions—"We interrupt this broadcast to bring you blah, blah, blah. . . . Three, two, one, we have a lift-off!"— but I developed a reputation for not being able to handle a war story. It was true. My twenty-second leads were unnaturally stilted. I had trouble writing two basic words. "The enemy."

To keep my values in a semblance of order, I embarked on a double life. I mailed contributions to the Fifth Avenue Peace Parade Committee, quaking in fear that my signature on the check would be used in some future Red-baiting inquisition, and I marched on weekends in the big antiwar demonstrations. One day at the office we got in a funny piece of film that was never going to air. At the close of an airport press conference (the usual light-at-the-end-of-the-tunnel stuff), General Westmoreland climbed the ladder to his plane, tripped on a top rung, and went sprawling. With absolutely no crack in his military demeanor, he got up, saluted, and climbed back up the steps. I made the film editor screen the clip for me over and over. Trip, sprawl, salute—it became my personal metaphor for the war.

One night my assignment was to prepare a clip of the president's press conference for the 11:00 feed. That evening LBJ had made one of his solemn announcements about resuming the bombing raids over Hanoi and Haiphong. You didn't need to be a genius to figure out which clip to use. Okay, you bastard, I thought, I can't stop you from bombing, but you're not going to say it on ABC. I chose another clip. My breech of professional conduct verged on sabotage. The next morning I heard muttering about my poor news judgment.

The week before the New Hampshire primary, I came to work wearing a McCarthy button. Eyebrows were raised. Real journalists didn't wear political buttons. ABC News was so unmindful of Gene McCarthy in New Hampshire that we hadn't even sent a reporter to cover the campaign. I looked around at my colleagues. I thought, not for the first time, *I don't belong here*. At some point between New Hampshire and the California primary, when Bobby Kennedy was murdered, I quit. Without realizing I was part of a surge of national alienation, I had joined the great upheaval of 1968.

For the next couple of years, while I found my way into the radical wing of the women's movement, I followed the war on my television set, like most other civilians. The most memorable stories did not originate with the big news organizations, they came to light via circuitous routes. The "tiger cages" on Con Son (Poulo Condore) Island—revealed to a congressional delegation by Don Luce, affiliated with the World Council of Churches. My Lai—pieced together by Seymour Hersh, working for an alternate news service.

As the war dragged on, I wasn't alone in my growing inattention to the specifics. Not many people I knew, even those who retained their establishment ties, had the stomach for specifics any longer. Acting on the diagnosis that America was a very sick country in need of radical change, I threw myself into feminist activism. It was a form of salvation. Others found it in Vietnam Veterans Against the War, the MOBE, the Black Panther Party, rock music, flower power, LSD, be-ins, group gropes, still others in an extreme political analysis that led by airtight logic to acts of violence. The frightening thing was, when you looked up from whatever it was you were doing, the war was still there.

And then, in quick succession, some images from Saigon in April 1975. A cargo plane, the first salvo in a humanitarian/propaganda gesture called Operation Babylift, crashes fourteen minutes after takeoff from Tan Son Nhut airport, spewing the broken bodies of a couple of hundred orphans over the terrain. There are mob scenes at the United States embassy as thousands of frantic Vietnamese pushing to get inside the compound are held back by marines. From a landing pad on the roof, relays of helicopters fly remaining embassy personnel and some faithful retainers to aircraft carriers waiting offshore. The same morning, the first NVA tanks ram through the wrought-iron gates of the presidential palace.

Maggie and I headed downstairs for lunch at the ex–Continental Shelf, remodeled to fit the changing times as Chez Guido, an air-conditioned Italian restaurant. The owner, Guido Cora, a voluble, ponytailed entrepreneur from Venice, recommended the baked green lasagne and cappuccino from his espresso machine.

The lasagne was excellent, the cappuccino was strong, the clientele was businessmen and tourists. From the shape of the room, its chandeliers and pilasters, I tried to imagine how it had looked at the turn of the century, when the men dressed like planters and the women wore hats and were corseted under their high-necked white gowns.

Guido had come to the restaurant business in Saigon via a

pizzeria in Zurich. He had married a Vietnamese woman, a circumstance that eased the way for his joint venture—a 60-40 split favoring the government—when such things became possible under the new freedoms of *doi moi*. Today, foreign investors are offered better terms in joint ventures, according to the amount of capital they put in. Chez Guido was the first Italian restaurant the town had seen in twenty years, but Guido was not without worries. Import regulations kept changing, a nerve-racking problem for his wine cellar.

Our host for the luncheon was Thomas Weigelt, vice director of the oil-services and tour agency in charge of our in-country arrangements. Thomas hailed from the former German Democratic Republic, and had met *his* Vietnamese wife in Moscow, when both were studying Soviet literature and economics on scholarships. His Saigon in-laws had welcomed the Communist regime in 1975, voluntarily turning over their spacious villa to the state in the rush of enthusiasm to abolish private property, reducing their living quarters to one floor while several families of strangers moved in upstairs. Now Thomas's in-laws were trying to get rid of the interlopers and reassert their ownership rights through a legal system that was struggling, as they were, to adjust to the changing times. They felt it wasn't fair that they should be penalized for trying to be good Communists in the previous decade while families that hadn't altered their bourgeois ways were positioned to make a fortune. Impressed by the success of Chez Guido, Thomas was wondering if a German rathskeller featuring beer and knockwurst in his in-laws' villa might go over big in the new Saigon.

Only when we had finished the meal and Thomas had sent us on our way with a warning to watch our purses—a needless suggestion to New York women—did I realize that we had spent most of the lunch talking about money.

"Ah," Thomas offered as an afterthought, "it is hard to believe that so many old Rolex watches are for sale in the city." Ho, Ho, Ho Chi Minh! Welcome to Saigon.

Saigon is not beautiful, nor is there much reason why it should be. It lacks the cool green parks and gemlike lakes of Hanoi, and its harbor is not one of those knockout natural curves like Hong Kong's or Sydney's that leaves you gasping. The imperial lines of boulevards laid out by the French are obscured by a hodgepodge of latter-day constructions destined for the wrecker's ball but gussied up for the present with Christmas tree lights, neon marquees, billboards that trumpet Sanyo, Panasonic, Sharp. In the last few years the population has swollen to over four million, matching its wartime bloat, most of the new influx migrants from Vietnam's populous northern provinces who came south looking for work.

If Hanoi is awakening to Stage 2, exchanging bicycles for scooters as the preferred means of transportation, Saigon is gaining on Stage 3, the private car, its privileged status denoted by a white license plate amid green plates for government vehicles and red plates for the military. For now, whole families chug by on sputtering motorbikes—Mom, Pop, and the kids balanced like circus performers—while sport-shirted young men and long-gloved young ladies, à la mode in dark glasses, zoom solo on heavy-duty Hondas. Dark elbow-length gloves are dernier cri for the fashion-conscious female motorcyclist, taking over where the sun parasol left off. High school girls, wearing the white ao dai, peddle in flotillas of conventional bicycles when classes let out, while grade schoolers of both sexes zip by in white shirts and red ties. Only naive tourists, their faces frozen in startled grins, allow themselves to be wheeled in old-fashioned cyclos through the lurching, snarled traffic.

The desire of the Saigonese to be part of the passing parade, or to relax in a bit of shade with a tall glass of something or other and watch the parade pass by, is matched by a mercantile lust that fifteen years of a hard socialist line couldn't extinguish. In Hanoi, it is said, you feel like a guest. In Saigon I felt like a prospect. Small boys were the worst offenders when it came to hawking, unresponsive to strictures of no, No, NO! It was impossible to walk two steps from the hotel without someone wanting to sell me a souvenir I didn't need—tintype postcards, poorly reproduced, of old Saigon, a *Miss Saigon* t-shirt, a *Good Morning, Vietnam* t-shirt, an End the Embargo Now t-shirt, a small, furry animal with big button eyes and no discernible tail that I believe was a pygmy slow loris.

Whatever it was, I'd never seen the likes of it before. The appealing little creature climbing over the shoulder of a street vendor on Dong Khoi was snapped up in a twinkle by a resident Japanese businessman who happened to stroll by. He had never seen anything like it before, either. The purchaser was given a wicker cage and a banana for his new pet. Transaction concluded, the vendor pulled two more lorises from her basket, one each for Maggie and me. We respectfully declined.

Nycticebus pygmaeus, the pygmy slow loris, is a nocturnal primate seven inches in length that is found only in the forests of Vietnam and Laos, which are rapidly depleting. Its diet includes insects and fruit. To the consternation of wildlife protectionists, the exotic animal trade, for eating and pet-keeping, flourishes openly in Saigon. Macaques, gibbons, and lorises are the backbone of the market. The loris is very cute. By now the Japanese businessman I met on Dong Khoi must be aware that it marks its range with urine.

*   *   *

Books have been written about the intrinsic differences between Northerners and Southerners, or between Easterners and Westerners, all over the globe. Vietnam is no exception to the rule that within one indivisible nation, geography and climate present certain objective conditions that inspire differing attitudes, temperaments, tastes in food, points of view. Hanoi has four seasons, including a cold winter. Saigon is hot and rainy or hot and dry. The historic character-building lesson of the North, necessitating eternal vigilance and collective struggle, was the fight to tame the Red River and a perpetual cycle of floods and drought. In the less populous, more recently settled South—a newcomer, ethnographically speaking—the mighty but gentler Mekong offered up its alluvial riches with less human effort and tribulation. Northerners developed a habit of looking over their shoulders at China, while Southerners often intermarried with the Khmers and the Chams.

Nothing in human temperament is graven in stone, but the Northerners, as the French found them, seemed more industrious, intellectual, and poetic, while the Southerners tended to be more relaxed, individualistic, and open to strangers and temporal pleasures. The conquerors achieved their goals first in the South, where they met with the least resistance. "Cochin China" was made an outright French colony in 1867. "Annam" and "Tonkin" were declared protectorates seventeen bitter years later. It was probably not happenstance that when things appeared to settle down, the French put their one university in Hanoi, their best museum in the central region, and their opium refinery in Saigon.

Fowler, the world-weary journalist of *The Quiet American*, was given to smoking a few pipes before retiring for the night, and his creator, Graham Greene, waxed romantic about Saigon dreaming in the pages of his autobiography,

Ways of Escape. Greene was very specific about how to cop in Saigon. In his day there was a code understood by every cyclo driver. You put your thumb in your mouth and made a gesture "rather like a long nose." After giving this sign, you'd be whisked to a *fumerie* in Cholon, the Chinese quarter. When I demonstrated the thumb-in-mouth and long-nose routine for a friend in my living room, he burst into laughter. "You try that in Saigon," he warned, "and they'll take you to a dentist." So I didn't. I was on a natural high in the city, anyway.

Opium was among the many ingenious devices by which the French made Vietnam profitable. Beyond the basic taxation system—a "head" tax on every male, a land tax on every *mau* (slightly less than an acre)—the colonizers had three government monopolies that together accounted for 70 percent of their operating revenues: salt, opium, and alcohol. It had been the custom, and still is today, for peasants to brew their own rice wine from the local harvest. Under the iron hand of Paul Doumer, the colonizers banned local winemaking and set up a system of informants who snitched on village distillers. To force the purchase of factory-bottled wine, each province was required by law to consume a fixed amount per month or per year.

Wine was basic to Vietnamese culture, but opium smoking had generally been confined to the clannish society of Chinese merchants and gamblers. After the French takeover, the crude resin of poppies grown by the Hmong in the hills of Laos was brought to Saigon, where a French-built refinery produced a quick-burning essence. Chinese middlemen bought in bulk and retailed the product through their *fumeries*, gambling dens, and private warehouses. As compradors, or agents of the government, they received a commission for collecting the opium taxes and did a brisk trade in smuggled opium on the side. Addiction rates in the Vietnamese population soared. The expedient of pumping the economy with drugs that blotted out reality and temporal pain had a ruinous parallel during our tenure in Indochina, when Saigon officials—the names Thieu and Ky were whispered—oversaw the heroin traffic that turned scores of thousands of South Vietnamese and American GIs into addicts.

Southerners today have a reputation for being seekers of wealth and profligate spenders compared to Northerners; after all, they cut their teeth on the seductive temptations of Western consumer culture during the war. The per capita income in Saigon and the fertile Mekong Delta is twice the national average. Although the region accounts for only one-quarter of the country's population, it produces half of Vietnam's rice, most of its seafood exports, and all of its exported oil. *Doi moi*'s innovations were tried out first in Saigon and the delta provinces before they became law in the North. In a situation that is not likely to change, according to Murray Hiebert, Hanoi bureau chief for the *Far Eastern Economic Review*, the North dominates politics while the South drives the economy.

Despite the rhetoric of "learn from," Hanoi's leaders, flushed with their military triumphs, felt they had nothing to learn from the South, where Saigonese capitalists had battened on war profits. For the first full decade of the reunified nation's existence, skilled entrepreneurs and tradespeople were scorned, successful private businesses were abolished, and individual freedoms were ignored. The urbane ethnic Chinese community, which had specialized in shopkeeping and moneylending, was encouraged to flee. Saigon's sophisticated banking system, based on the French model, was dismantled. The personal check became a relic; gold and hard currency were hoarded at home. The swift and clumsy imposition of Northern-style socialism sent shock waves through the middle-class intellectuals in the Provisional Revolutionary Government who had worked underground in the belly of the beast during the war. Believing they had been "squeezed like a lemon" by Northern ideologues who never intended to share the power or give them a voice, many stalwarts quietly retired from politics or went into exile.

Now, in a stunning reversal, the government is reinventing the wheel. The lurching shift to a market economy, proceeding by stops and starts, is being guided by Premier Vo Van Kiet, an old Viet Minh warrior who remained in the South during the American war, living in safe houses and traveling in secret as the Communist Party secretary for Saigon and environs. (This radical Southerner has impeccable revolutionary credentials; his wife and children were killed in a B-52 attack when they were visiting him at a forest hideout.) Following the pattern that leaders of developing countries seem to prefer when they get on the market-economy track, democratic reforms lag behind.

After the sudden collapse of the Soviet Union, Asian business interests rushed in to replace Eastern Europe as Vietnam's major trading partners. Ideological barriers seemed to disappear overnight as entrepreneurs from Singapore, Japan, Hong Kong, Taiwan, South Korea, Thailand, Indonesia, and Malaysia arrived at the door of the former pariah in the quest for profit, drawn by an educated, relatively skilled labor force used to low wages, and encouraged by a liberal investment policy that on paper was the most generous in Asia. Patiently they worked their way through the labyrinthine government ministries in Hanoi for official approvals while they settled in Saigon to do business.

In an interesting twist of fate, the rush to invest was pioneered by overseas Chinese, many of them longtime Vietnam residents before their forced departure as Boat People a decade earlier, at the height of the antagonism with China. Uniquely versed in conducting business within a mobile, loosely structured mode, the new entrepreneurs set up a clutch of garment factories and small-assembly shops, often with hand-me-down machinery from Vietnam's prosperous Asian neighbors. France and Australia were the first non-Asian countries to step in, followed by Germany and the Scandinavian countries. By 1992, the United States trade embargo had lost international support and become a unilateral action, a source of some merriment to investors from other nations.

Low-end production lines for shoes, textiles, and garments are often notorious for nineteenth-century sweatshop conditions. Grateful for the work, the prideful Vietnamese were nonetheless dismayed by some of the foreigners' methods, which amounted to rough-and-tumble exploitation. Walkouts and wildcat strikes, unheard of in Communist countries, became another new wrinkle for the socialist republic. In one case, the South Korean manager of a Saigon luggage factory was called upon to apologize publicly for hitting his workers.

Most mornings at the Continental's breakfast garden I checked in with a team of three Canadian businessmen who had begun to test the joint-venture waters. "Vietnam is the rising star of Southeast Asia, the best example of positive change," said one. "These are people who understand prosperity. They have some prior knowledge of it." The Canadians were eyeing a piece of property across the Saigon River, close to the port, where they hoped to build a plant for the manufacture of tractor-trailers. At odd hours I'd catch a glimpse of them wearily conducting negotiations with their Vietnamese counterparts at an ornate table in the hotel lobby. Their tractor-trailer proposal was moving more slowly than they desired.

Another of my fellow guests was an exuberant fellow from Royal Dutch Shell. This Dutch and British cartel had won a major lease for oil exploration rights off the coast of Vung Tau, as had British Petroleum and some French, Japanese, and Malaysian competitors. "Tell your countrymen the major blocks have already been allocated," he gleefully teased. "The bets have been laid." He presented me with two baseball caps embossed with the Shell logo. Oh well. I passed them on to the pleasant hall porter who took care of the laundry.

Mobil and American Shell discovered Saigon's offshore oil too late in the war to do them much good. A Vietnamese-Soviet joint venture took over development of the Bach Ho (White Tiger) field after the Americans departed. Production reached a hundred thousand barrels of crude per day a decade later. By then the Russians had run out of money and the Western companies had been invited back in. Oil exploration is Vietnam's largest and hottest investment sector, with Bach Ho, Dai Hung (Big Bear), and Thanh Long (Blue Dragon) the fields to be reckoned with. Broken Hill Proprietary, the Australian giant, is among the internationals leading the scramble. Handicapped by the embargo, at least six American companies got a late start in the race and now may have to "farm in" on another company's concession. Natural gas has also been found in quantity off Vietnam's coast. There is heady talk of a gas pipeline, an oil refinery, a chance for Vietnam to double its GDP on oil alone. There is also talk of the contested fields that lie between Vietnam, Malaysia, and China, and of the inevitable oil spills down the line.

My direct participation in capitalism is usually confined to shopping. Ben Thanh Market, a cavernous building just a short walk down Le Loi Boulevard from the hotel, is a mecca for the entire country. "You-can-get anything you-want . . . " Oh, Arlo! The trouble was, I didn't need bolts of silk, cotton, or polyester, huge quantities of rice, tea, and other foodstuffs, hardware, pots and pans, aluminum furniture, shirts and pants. But it's hard not to get in the swim. On a spree, I bought a dozen plastic molds for sweetened bean curd desserts that maybe I could use for Jell-O. Next I loaded up on Vietnamese coffee beans, considered among the world's finest. Periodically, shipments of Vietnamese coffee, labeled "Product of Thailand," are confiscated by U.S. customs. After this purchase it dawned on me that I'd added several pounds to my luggage and no one I knew had a coffee grinder.

Next I spotted the purveyor of Bat Trang ceramics and bought one of her pots.

"My name is My," she said, writing it on a slip of paper. She pronounced it "Me." "You know My?" she asked. "You My."

My is also the Vietnamese word for "American."

I squatted next to her on the floor, surrounded by the familiar pots and bowls. We were My and My. She indicated her pleasure by stirring the air around me with a paper fan, and said she was studying English with another Ben Thanh merchant so they'd be ready when the Americans came back. Her friend came hurrying over. Then My's husband arrived. I was a celebrity. Across the way, a team of uniformed butchers was scaling the tough skins off sides of pork with metal scrapers. Near the butchers, a covey of women sat thigh by thigh, in astonishing intimacy, their skirts hiked up, getting their toenails clipped and painted. "You-can-get anything you-want . . . "

Later I returned to Dong Khoi, the former Catinat. It begins at a lively square, a broad intersection where Saigon's own Notre Dame Cathedral, red brick and spired, the building materials brought over from France, vies for attention with the iron-framed and glass-domed central post office, mellowed to verdigris. A preserved Belle Epoque jewel with ceiling fans, arched lampposts, and pastepots for affixing stamps, the post office has a window for the DHL courier service and displays a large, romantic portrait of Ho Chi Minh, one of several in the city that officially bears his name. From the intersection—known as John F. Kennedy Square during our war—Dong Khoi proceeds south to the Saigon River.

The street turned out to be much shorter than I expected, but it was chockablock with uneven signs of change. Between the Continental and the Majestic, the well-worn trail of Graham Greene, several high-priced restaurants for tourists have taken root, planted among souvenir shops, gem stores, and lacquerware outlets.

The pickings in the souvenir shops were slender for an American with dollars—polished tortoiseshell and carved ivory that wouldn't get through U.S. customs, small unset rubies and sapphires. I spent two dollars for a heart-shaped box in luminous overlays of golden brown, a traditional shade of lacquer the Vietnamese inelegantly but aptly call "wing of the cockroach." The cockroach box was one of only three gift items I could bring myself to buy in Saigon without lowering my standards. My other prizes were a cunning paper snake that danced on a string, its wriggling body made of recycled newsprint, and a Coke-can Huey with whirring propellers and a sliding door. The street vendor on Lam Son Square who sold me the Huey (four dollars, no bargaining) carried a worn manual of American planes in case anyone doubted the authenticity of his soda-can models.

Except for these purchases, and the loris, there was a boring consistency to Dong Khoi's wares: piles of metal dog tags,

Zippo lighters etched with a place name—Chu Lai, Ben Tre, Bien Hoa—and a motto like "No Hope Without Dope," antique watches in the hundreds bearing the logos of Rolex, Patek Philippe, Bulova, Longines, Piaget.

In a repeat of Hanoi, Maggie and I watched two British travelers pick up a pair of Rolexes for one hundred dollars. Something was definitely wrong. At the next shop we visited, a young woman named Lan spilled the beans. We didn't twist her arm or anything. She was smitten by Maggie.

"You know the dog tags are fake?" she giggled.

"Yes, Lan, we do."

"You know the Zippos are fake?"

"Yes. They're probably real Zippos, but they're not left over from the America era."

Lan giggled some more. "You know that you buy the Rolex in America for four thousand dollars?" She was on the verge of hysteria. "Vietnamese very clever people!" she roared.

"Yes, Lan, we have reason to know that, too."

The watches were nameless Swiss imports that underwent skillful cosmetic surgery before they were put out for sale. With that cleared up, Lan directed us to a shop around the corner where the shelves were loaded with perfectly plausible bottles of fake Chanel perfume.

Fakery has reached epidemic proportions in Vietnam, and it isn't restricted to "bargains" fobbed off on greedy, gullible tourists. *Nuoc mam*, liquor, beer, antibiotics, soap, chemical fertilizers, insecticides, cigarettes, cement, and small appliances may not be what the packaging says. Some ruses are dangerous, but some are funny, as in the case of the manager of a state cigarette factory whose brand was a dud with consumers. He simply repackaged his smokes with labels of another state-owned factory's popular brand. A milk-pasteurizing plant found a readier market by distilling an imitation lemon liqueur after closing hours. Halida, a joint venture with Carlsberg, the Danish beer company, accused another brewery of collecting discarded Halida cans and refilling them with its inferior brew. The fresh pop-top seals were well-nigh perfect.

There is an arresting photograph in Saigon's Museum of the Revolution that I've never seen reproduced elsewhere. At first you wonder what's so remarkable about three haystacks in a field. Then you notice a pair of legs under each haystack. The photo was taken during Tet 1968. The haystacks are three Viet Cong fighters. *Till Birnam wood remove to Dunsinane.*

Probably not many American officers in MACV (Military Assistance Command, Vietnam) were acquainted with *Macbeth,* but they were surprised time and again—flabbergasted is more like it—by adversaries who could camouflage their positions so successfully, reload spent shell casings with fresh powder, or fashion a rifle out of odd parts, some galvanized pipe, and a homemade wooden bolt. An ingenious talent for taking a thing apart, capturing its essence, and copying it with whatever discarded materials were at hand was a crucial skill in the wars of liberation. I found it depressing to see that talent, and that irrepressible spirit, employed in the service of a fraudulent pop-top, a fake dog tag, or an imitation Rolex. On the brighter side, there is a long, honorable tradition of fakery in species survival, and furthermore, I can recall the silly postwar fakes that turned "Made in Japan" into a joke until the Japanese put their adaptive skills to work improving the design of German cameras.

I was musing on those haystacks one morning on the rooftop of the Rex Hotel, which quartered U.S. Army bachelor officers during the war. The rooftop was a favorite hang-

out for officers, the press corps, and civilian American con-
tractors, who barbecued steaks and baked potatoes on charcoal grills. Next door was a movie theater that was always
being evacuated because of bomb scares. In the adjoining
building, MACV conducted the daily press briefings known
as the Five O'Clock Follies. Late in the war, the Rex Dance
Hall, a sleazy pleasure dome on the ground floor, became a
favorite gathering place of Saigon's demimonde.

Now the government-owned enterprise was pushing hard
to be the premier hostelry in the city, breathing down the
neck of the Continental, also government-owned, but facing
stiff competition from such sleek new joint ventures as the
Century (Hong Kong money) and the Norfolk (Australian).
Deluxe hotels are springing up in Saigon like mushrooms.
Pinched for space on historic Le Loi Boulevard, the Rex borrowed the Museum of the Revolution courtyard across the
street for an outdoor cafe. Since the museum occupies the
former mansion of the French lieutenant governor, white-
jacketed waiters serve drinks in a formal parterre where a
Huey, a tank, and an F-5 jet peep through a tangle of vines
and flowers.

Despite such attractions, the museum cafe wasn't a great
draw. Day and night, the action at the Rex was still on its
rooftop, where another fantastic juxtaposition of images was
easier on the emotions. The barbecue grills were gone. In
their place, potted tamarinds, plaster elephants, a stuffed
boar, and a crouched wooden Indian shooting a bow vied for
attention with a miniature waterfall, tropical fish tanks, and
twittering birds in cages. Behind the bar, a daisy-wheel
printer, probably one of the first in Saigon, contributed its
whir to the cacophony of the birds. At dusk, twinkling
Christmas tree lights and an illuminated revolving crown,

the Rex logo, added more glitz to the show. Suspecting that a great wit was behind such a kitschy display, I went to the source.

As I was talking with Dao Huu Loan, the Rex hotel's manager, it occurred to me, belatedly, that kitsch is in the mind of the beholder. "I was re-creating the rain forest of central Vietnam," Mr. Loan said severely. The rest of our conversation took the form of a quiz. A transplanted Northerner who adapted to free-market competition with undisguised relish, Mr. Loan wanted to know how the Rex stacked up against the hotels that had won my patronage. After we took a tour of the Rex tailor shop—the finest, he said, in the city—he dropped the news that Senator John Kerry would be checking in that afternoon.

I wasn't the only one with the scoop. About twenty of us were on hand to witness Senator Kerry's arrival, including a few real working reporters—a woman from Reuters, an ABC News crew, and a fellow from a Massachusetts newspaper who was traveling with the senator's party. Independent of one another, some of us had bought End the Embargo Now t-shirts to wave or wear or give to the senator at an appropriate moment.

The senator was late. The press contingent got rather giddy. More End the Embargo Now t-shirts appeared. When Kerry alighted from his car, the welcome took on the tumultuous aspect of a political demonstration. Flashback to the sixties. I just couldn't help myself. "End the embargo now!" I shouted.

John Kerry was not amused. The former navy lieutenant and activist with Vietnam Veterans Against the War was weary and guarded. He had come from a week of exacting negotiations in Hanoi on the MIA question. He had come from *years* of fact-finding commissions, reports, and negotiations on the MIAs and the trade embargo. At the fever pitch of the antiwar movement, when radicalized veterans marched on Washington and hurled their medals over the White House fence, exerting a moral force unprecedented in the annals of warfare, who would have predicted that their energy would dissipate and their voices fade, and that it would be conservative veterans who organized themselves, rallying around the MIA/POW banner and offering stiff, continuing, emotional opposition to normalizing relations with Vietnam twenty years later. Or that a guilt-ridden, shamed nation unable to offer its dispirited returning fighters a hero's welcome would take its moral guidance in the following decades from the conservative vets and the MIA families, unwilling to hurt them further. Kerry had stayed on course, using an establishment career to push his political vision. I felt like an idiot.

That evening at Chez Guido, when the senator's party of ten arrived for pasta and scaloppine, I had a chance to make a fool of myself a second time.

"Hello there, I'm the one who . . . I forgot to say that I know your sister. . . ."

Warily he shook my hand and returned to his dinner.

More well-heeled travelers pass through Saigon, where they can expect to find the familiar comforts, than anywhere else in the country. Gone are the days when Madame Dai's law library, its glass-enclosed cabinets stocked with musty leatherbound French tomes, was the only place in town for a decent French meal. An Australian tour group was trundling through her famous villa, hoping for a glimpse of the crusty old lawyer renowned for her outspoken opinions, on the night we arrived to claim our reservations. Madame Dai, alas, had overbooked. After a half-hour wait with four other disgruntled customers, we departed in a huff when we were shown to a table hastily set up in the hallway. At the crisply designed City Grill on Dong Khoi, the inspiration of a young Vietnamese who'd lived in the States, the cuisine was California nouvelle, the drinks were Margaritas and Harvey Wall-bangers, and the music was "Jambalaya," performed by a string band. A distressed maître d' flew over when Maggie set up her tripod. "Please, madam," he wailed. "You are destroying my ambience." Chastened, the photographer applied herself to the mesquite chicken.

On Thomas Weigelt's recommendation, we had a meal at Thanh Nien, a charming indoor-outdoor Vietnamese restaurant where the clientele was young, hip, and local. *Thanh nien*, meaning "youth," was the name that Ho Chi Minh gave to his revolutionary youth league and political journal in the 1920s. The journal *Thanh Nien* espoused revolutionary nationalism and Communist theory, and was required reading for liberation-minded Vietnamese intellectuals in its day. The restaurant Thanh Nien caters to decorous Saigonese intellectuals of the new generation who sit around the piano bar listening to Mozart and jazz.

As in Hanoi, after we had our fill of the fancy places, we went down alleys and up flights of stairs seeking out the "dusty rice" establishments where the regular folk ate.

Our driver and our guide in Saigon had good memories of the Americans. Sobersided Thanh (pronounced "Tang"), who was my age, had worked as a garage mechanic for "You-said," the U.S. Agency for International Development. He had not been sent to a reeducation camp after 1975—most likely, he believed, because he had not been in a sensitive position. Tuyen (pronounced "Twen"), the son of an ARVN colonel who died in combat, was in his early thirties and remembered the war only vaguely. "Really," he insisted, "it

swirled around us. We were not very aware as schoolboys."
The two men were very courtly, verging on overprotective.
Spending time with them was like being on a chaste double
date.

Together we found the street in Cholon where fifteen-
year-old Marguerite Duras kept her assignations with her
Chinese lover—in the movie, that is. There was no mistak-
ing the alley of blue-shuttered doors where the exteriors were
shot, and shopkeepers told us how the film crew dumped red
earth over the pavement to transport the locale back to
1930. Little else had required a touch-up in timeless Cholon.
The trading quarter, a jumble of canals, shops, and temples,
was booming again, thanks to the new relaxations. While
Maggie photographed the street arcades from a balcony, I
happily browsed at ground level. Gold chains bought and
sold by weight, pyramids of coffee beans, tea leaves and rice
graded by aroma and color, hogs by the haunch, "thousand-
year-old" eggs packed in clay for a mere twenty days till they
reached the bilious shade of green that announced them
scrumptious.

The Lover, Duras's lyric novel about her childhood in a
family of failed colonials, had been faithfully transposed to
the screen by Jean-Jacques Annaud, who filmed all the exte-
rior sequences in-country, unlike the director of *Indochine*,
who jigsawed landscapes of the Philippines and Malaysia in
the great tradition of the spaghetti Western. *The Lover* was a
big hit when it played in Saigon, the sensual attraction
between European girl and Asian man proving as delightfully
provocative in 1992 as when the teenage Duras had claimed
her rebellious freedoms six decades earlier. Fashion-conscious
jeune filles showed their appreciation by making Duras's prized
totem, as worn by actress Jane March—a flat-brimmed fedora
circled by a broad band of ribbon—a sartorial trend. I tried

on several models at an outdoor stall. Too small for my American head.

My route into the Mekong Delta had been plotted by Duras. Or rather, it seemed like a nice idea to cross a branch of the Mekong on the Vinh Long ferry near Sa Dec, the outpost where her ruined, half-mad mother taught in a "native school," and then push on to Dong Thap province and the Plain of Reeds, where I'd heard of a sanctuary for sarus cranes that could be reached from the river port of Cao Lanh.

Tuyen didn't know of the bird reserve. Thanh consulted other drivers and reported that the road past Cao Lanh was unpaved and frequently flooded.

The following morning we set off.

Of all the world's rivers that resonate with romance, conquest, warfare, human migration and suffering, few command more respect than the Mekong. The snaking giant flows for 2,600 miles, from the Tibetan highlands through China down to Burma and Laos, forming the border between those two countries, then nicks a piece of Thailand and courses through Cambodia, where it is joined at Phnom Penh by the waters of the Tonle Sap and soon enters Vietnam, branching into seven tributaries that twist and sprawl across the soggy lowlands southwest of Saigon until they empty into the South China Sea. The patchwork of fields dissected by canals, dikes, and irrigation ditches is so naturally fertile with rich alluvial soil that three crops of rice can be harvested a year.

During the American war, the delta was designated as IV Corps, or the Fourth Military Region, in MACV jargon, a Viet Cong stronghold targeted for B-52 carpet bombing, search-and-destroy missions, tons of napalm and chemical defoliants, and "pacification"—those barbed-wire enclaves called strategic hamlets, ours during the day, theirs at night. The muddy rice flats, reedy marshlands, and mangrove swamps crisscrossed by waterways in the back areas miles from the primitive road network made hospitable guerrilla hideouts. A joint army-navy project, the Mobile Riverine Force, patrolled the coastal and inland waterways in fiber glass gunboats; the VC used sampans. For U.S. ground troops, a stint in the delta was the most demoralizing assignment in the war. Fragging, the murder of an overzealous officer by rolling a hand grenade toward his sleeping quarters, began here.

The delta's prominence in the war petered out toward the end. Hanoi's military strategists knew, as did the panicky Saigon generals, that once Saigon toppled, the delta would fall swiftly. But damage to the region in the previous decade had been horrific. Agent Orange and the other sprays turned out to have deadlier effects in the southern coastal regions than elsewhere in the country. Tidal mangroves—the towering leathery-leafed evergreens that spread their arching roots above the soil like the flying buttresses of Gothic cathedrals—proved more susceptible than other tree species to chemical defoliants. A single application could do them in. Half of the delta's mangrove forests were destroyed, upsetting the fragile ecosystem, accelerating erosion of tidal soils, depleting plant and animal life.

Some of the denuded mangrove swamps are a total loss, ghostly places that are stagnant breeding grounds for malaria-bearing mosquitoes. The locals call them Agent Orange museums. But other stretches have undergone a natural regeneration, along with substantial reforestation efforts. It's doubtful that Vietnam's mangrove forests will ever be what they were. Shrimp farming in cleared ponds is easier and more profitable than coddling trees.

During the Pol Pot nightmare, Cambodian refugees fleeing the Khmer Rouge settled in the recovering region, to which no doubt they felt some affinity. On maps drawn before the eighteenth century, much of the watery land belonged to the Cambodian kingdom.

The sun was shining on the rice fields as we drove along at a leisurely pace, stopping to admire a Cao Dai temple on the side of the road. The delta is studded with phantasmagoric Cao Dai temples, each with an all-seeing divine eye over its portal.

An odd religion founded in the 1920s by a Vietnamese civil servant to unify the teachings of Buddhism, Taoism, Confucianism, and Christianity, Cao Dai (pronounced "Cow's Eye") proceeded to capture the imagination of masses of poor southern peasants with opulent pageantry and intimate séances, and an eclectic pantheon of saints—Lao Tse, Joan of Arc, Shakespeare, Sun Yat-sen, and Victor Hugo among them. Its converts were vegetarian and its priests, male and female, were celibate. The Cao Dai Holy See administered its own territory in the border province of Tay Ninh and maintained a private army, to the frustration of the French and Japanese occupiers in their day. Graham Greene did a colorful set piece on the Cao Dai in *The Quiet American*. In 1955, as Greene's novel was being published in England and America—where it would get stomped in *The New Yorker* by A.J. Liebling, who didn't appreciate the tone—Ngo Dinh Diem was bringing the Cao Daists to heel in the delta with CIA help. Adding luster to his image, Diem went on to subdue the Hoa Hao, another syncretic faith in the delta with its own private army. That was his "miracle man" phase. Special Forces recruited warriors from the two broken sects as mercenaries in the Civilian Irregular Defense Group program, giving them the task of routing the Viet Cong from remote hilltop pagodas, but a number eventually joined the guerrillas they were being paid to crush. Cao Dai appears to be making a comeback in the South, albeit under government supervision. Some sources guess there may be two million adherents today.

Before we knew it, we had driven onto the Vinh Long ferry, where Marguerite Duras first laid eyes on her rich Chinese lover. Our crossing seemed straight out of that colonial era, except that our vehicle of privilege was an air-conditioned white Nissan made in Japan, not a French-made black Léon-Bollée, and the watery stretch that Duras liked to call the Plain of the Birds was birdless. A few wild birds were fluttering resignedly on deck, eight to a hand, in the clutch of a vendor who offered them to us but didn't really expect to make a sale. To buy a wild bird and release it is a way of acquiring merit for the afterlife in Buddhist belief. The hordes of child beggars plying the ferry had more temporal concerns. One little girl with blond hair, possibly a second-generation Amerasian, got to my heart and my pocketbook before her older mates shoved her aside, crying, in a frantic melee.

Vinh Long is the capital of Vinh Long province. Ngo Dinh Diem's older brother was the province's Catholic bishop before he became archbishop of Hue; during the Diem regime, rallies in support of the government were held on command. In the early sixties the province chief of Vinh Long was assassinated in broad daylight by Viet Cong guerrillas. During Tet 1968 the fighting in the provincial capital lasted five days, abated, and erupted once more. The downtown section was strewn with corpses. Most of the inhabitants fled to the countryside, and returned to find smoldering ruins. Vinh Long fought well in the final push, according to General Van Tien Dung in *Our Great Spring Victory: An*

Account of the Liberation of South Vietnam. It has been rebuilt since the war. A riverside park displayed the usual collection of American armaments. Kids played giddyap on a cannon, engaged us in peekaboo under a chopper, agreed to be treated to a cup of rice pudding. The war museum was closed.

We elected to stay in the car with the windows rolled up during the return trip by ferry. At lunchtime we reached the port of Cao Lanh, where we were sobered by the size of the stone-and-concrete memorial that was typically inscribed, "The Fatherland Will Not Forget You." Cao Lanh's revolutionary history harked back to May Day 1930, when a peasant insurrection spread to other delta provinces, creating havoc for six weeks before it was crushed by the French.

A new hotel, the My Tra, had a welcoming stucco facade and plantings of red-hot celosia and orange coreopsis. It looked like a promising place to spend the night. Large cases of beer and Coca-Cola were being unloaded in the empty lobby. I took a key from the uncertain receptionist and went to my room. The sole decoration on the wall was a girlie picture.

The route to the garden restaurant passed a row of cubicles where glassy-eyed, scantily clad young women were giving each other pedicures. We exchanged a few pleasantries. Between self-conscious giggles they told me they worked "upstairs."

It is hard not to stare when you're having lunch in a brothel. Sullen youths played billiards in the shade of a carport. A hawker came by with a tray of fried sweet bananas. A government official, identified as such by Tuyen from his semi-military attire, reclined like a young pasha under a coconut-palm umbrella as two hostesses attempted to pour his beer and serve his rice in the manner of geishas—probably the My Tra Hotel's creative response to *doi moi*. He gave them encouraging nods while meeting my gaze with a look that warned, "Don't tread on me." The women averted their eyes.

"Go ahead," I said to Maggie. "I dare you. Take out your camera." The photographer declined.

I had not expected to find that prostitution was one of the growth industries in the new Vietnam, but this was the second time it had intruded upon my field of vision. A reasonably sophisticated traveler is prepared to see entrepreneurial ladies of the night in brash big cities like Saigon, where foreign tourists and businessmen create a market. But in the roadside restaurant at Dong Ha, where Duy tried to pass off a tableful of tarted-up women as kitchen workers, and in Cao Lanh at the My Tra, I'd stumbled upon places catering to the local trade. The raw newness of it in a society that had proclaimed the eradication of the traffic in women twenty years ago made it that much more disturbing. More disturbing still to find it in the shadow of the monument: "The Fatherland Will Not Forget You."

During the war, the U.S. military, abetted by local officials, had fostered prostitution, as I detailed in *Against Our Will*. By 1966 the army's First Cavalry at An Khe, the First Infantry at Lai Khe, and the Fourth Infantry at Pleiku had each constructed a military brothel inside the barbed-wire perimeter of their base camps. Young women, often sold by their fathers, were recruited from outlying villages by greedy province chiefs who took a commission. They were escorted to the camps by local mayors who were in on the cut, and checked weekly for VD by army medics whose job was to keep down the incidence of sexually transmitted disease. The jaded legions of South Vietnamese prostitutes with their bouffant hairdos, heavy makeup, and silicone-injected breasts were pathetic emblems of a fractured society that had lost its moorings. In startling contrast, the revolutionaries put forward a stirring image of clean-scrubbed, fresh-faced women fighters loading an antiaircraft gun, guarding a captured American pilot, pointing their rifles toward the menace in the sky.

By conservative estimate, two hundred thousand full-time prostitutes in the South were left without a calling when the Americans departed. The socialist liberation government spoke glowingly and high-mindedly of rehabilitation projects, training schools in basketry and weaving, to teach the victims of American imperialism new skills. Prostitutes are accustomed to quick money, and I've yet to see one who found her salvation in weaving baskets, but that wasn't the point. The new society was addressing the evil; it appeared to be taking a moral stand. Above all, it was acknowledging its debt to the "long-haired army," the girls and women on the Ho Chi Minh Trail and in the delta swamplands who had fought so bravely alongside their men. For of all the special factors that enabled this small underdeveloped nation to defeat the technological might of the world's greatest power—unifying leaders, brilliant tacticians, a two-thousand-year-old tradition of guerrilla warfare inseparable from a passionate devotion to the land—ultimately it was women who made the difference. Without the women it could not have been done.

There is an old Vietnamese saying, "When the aggressor comes, women also fight." Vietnam is one of the few countries to honor the women who have participated in its historic struggles for independence, from the celebrated Trung sisters, who led an insurrection against the Chinese in A.D. 40, to a pair of modern revolutionaries who were instrumental in the Southern struggle: Nguyen Thi Dinh, a deputy commander of the Viet Cong, and Nguyen Thi Binh, known in the West as Madame Binh, who represented the Provisional Revolutionary Government at the Paris Peace Talks. But another twist on the theme of woman as heroic savior, one that is more conventional, runs parallel to inspiring tales of warrior women. It is exemplified by *The Tale of Kieu*, an early-nineteenth-century saga by Nguyen Du that is the most revered verse-novel in Vietnamese literature, wept over by romantics and claimed as a bible by conservatives and radicals alike.

Kieu, a clever, beautiful daughter in a family of scholars, rescues her father from debtors' prison and saves the family honor by going out into the cruel world to sell her body. After a fifteen-year odyssey of sexual exploitation along the lines of *Fanny Hill*, she is reunited with her betrothed, who in the meanwhile has married her younger sister. As an act of forgiveness, she is taken into his family as a platonic First Wife. Most Vietnamese can recite long sections of *The Tale of Kieu* by heart.

Friedrich Engels proposed that the status of women is the best barometer of a country's development. I mention him with rue, for it has become terribly apparent in the post-Communist era that volatile efforts to overhaul unworkable economic systems and attract foreign investment go hand in hand with an unsubtle retooling of the role and image of women. A traveler goes to Peking or Hanoi or Moscow or Prague and notes that the women are dressing more colorfully, a pleasing sign (who could object?) that the country is loosening its authoritarian restraints. Next, calendars and tourist brochures featuring buxom young women with come-hither smiles and prerevolutionary attire put in an appearance, followed by beauty contests and an influx of imported pornography. Finally and inescapably, battalions of young recruits, so new at the trade that their shame is more evident than their seductive skills, are dragooned into selling their bodies for quick gain.

It was painful to see this happening in Vietnam, and to recognize it as a retraction of ideals. A country that jailed political critics and put dissident Buddhists under house arrest (in August 1993 the human rights organization Asia Watch listed a score of Vietnamese religious and political dissidents who were under detention) seemed unable to prevent the rising tide of prostitution, just as it seemed powerless to stop the trade in illegally felled logs.

The excuse could not hold that the trade in women was strictly the result of foreign business pressure. True, among the Asian economic tigers that Vietnam was seeking to emulate, South Korea and Taiwan routinely used sexual services to clinch deals, and Thailand's sad reputation for sex tours was known the world over. But Vietnam's new trade catered primarily to local port workers and truck drivers, restless, underemployed, macho young men only recently demobilized from military service.

Enough history has passed before our eyes in the twentieth century to trace certain patterns. Socialist countries that fight hard for their freedoms never know quite what to do with their women in the aftermath of revolution. In Vietnam, most of the Communist Party's female stalwarts were shunted into the Women's Union, a parallel organization established in 1930. When male and female comrades got together at meetings, the female comrades served the tea. In beleaguered Cuba back in the sixties, Fidel Castro once scolded the women's organizations that were articulating their aspirations and demanding more rights; the time had come, he announced, for them to return to their homes and take up their traditional work again. No such pronouncements issued from the government of Vietnam, as far as I know, but friendly foreign scholars grumpily observed, usually in a footnote to whatever it was they were studying, that there were fewer women in high government positions than there had been during the war.

From various bits of evidence collected here and there, I came to my own conclusions. Battlefield deaths numbering perhaps two million had left the devastated reunified nation with what is awkwardly alluded to as a surplus of women. Older than the traditional age for marriage, unable to find partners, single women still in their prime had waged a four-year campaign, unreported in the international press, to force a sexually prudish government to grant them the legal right to bear children without benefit of matrimony. Vietnam's population soared after the war, as well it should have, but amid the rising birth rates duly recorded by government census takers, a watchful observer could discern a disturbing trend. Live births of males outnumbered live births of females by a ratio of 106 to 100. With no hard evidence of the kind that has been reported in China, one can only speculate with great reluctance that infanticide and/or discriminatory child-rearing practices favoring boy children lie behind the skewed rates.

Six months after I returned from Vietnam, I read a newspaper interview with Dr. Duong Quyn Hoa, a Communist organizer of the South's pro–Viet Cong intelligentsia during the war. Dr. Hoa, who served as health minister for the National Liberation Front/PRG, had given birth to a son in a forest hideout in 1970; the infant had succumbed to malaria. A decade earlier she had spent time in prison. Such hardships had been accepted then as the price one had to pay for liberation. Now, after years of silence, Dr. Hoa was speaking out against the regime she had helped bring into being, describing the injured child prostitutes she treated at her hospital as a manifestation of the new corruption. "We fought for freedom, independence and social justice," she said. "Now it is all money. You can count on your fingers the revolutionaries who still believe in ideals."

After the unexpectedly disquieting lunch, we set off again for the bird sanctuary, badly misjudging the traveling time. The road past Cao Lanh was not only unpaved but badly rutted as it stretched toward infinity, lined on both sides by thatch-and-wood houses, sometimes on stilts, with rickety bridges of logs and branches spanning a muddy watercourse running parallel to the road. On it went: a never-ending village of wall-to-wall humanity, with peasants tending to mats of rice drying on the roadside, chickens crossing the path, children playing, women preparing a meal, shirtless men in green army pants that indicated the presence of a nearby base, a water buffalo in harness, a cart loaded with pigs, a lactating dog, teams of bicycles, a roaring scooter, a lumbering bus (probably of East German origin but freshly repainted with the legend "DeSoto" in fond nostalgia for things American), a modest stand selling cigarettes and soda.

When Tuyen would inquire how far it was to the bird sanctuary, the answer was always "twenty kilometers on." Once it was "seven kilometers," and we visibly brightened, and then it was "twenty kilometers" again.

It was dark when we reached Tam Nong, a lively settlement in a New Economic Zone, and learned that the bird sanctuary was across the bridge. We were fifteen miles from the Cambodian border. Obviously we would not be returning to our rooms at the My Tra bordello that evening. What we didn't know was that it would have been quicker and easier to reach our destination by boat.

Crossing the bridge, we drove through a muddy field to the

one certain beacon, a lighted, substantial house. I groggily wondered if they'd have to take us in. The sanctuary's director, who greeted us in his pajamas, seemed to be having the same thought. "This happens all the time," he said with a shrug.

The name of the sanctuary was Tram Chim, which means "bird swamp." We were offered tea after we agreed to return to the nearby town for the night. At 6:00 a.m., if we wished, we could go out in a launch and cruise through some of the reserve's fifteen thousand hectares (roughly forty-five thousand acres). The bad news was that we'd arrived a month too early to see the migrating cranes. The eastern sarus—a five-foot-tall red-headed bird—alights at Tram Chim in late December and stays through April, the dryest of the dry season, when it can walk around sociably, ankle-deep in water, digging tuberous sedges from the mud. Plenty of other birds, the director assured us, could be observed at daybreak. Before we departed, he took us to an exhibition room. Posters from the International Crane Foundation and a picture of founder George Archibald were on the wall.

We returned to Tam Nong for a late dinner at an outdoor table in front of a row of video cafes. The din was infernal. People seemed buoyant; the rainy season was ending. With its unpaved town center rigged up with electric lights and jammed with food stalls to accommodate the passing throngs of men, women, and children, Tam Nong had the look of a revivalist encampment, although the hopes being revived in this New Economic Zone were for a decent living.

Thanh carefully wiped our chopsticks and swirled tea in our cups to give them a good cleaning.

"He's more worried about the sanitation than you are," Tuyen joked.

After a restless night in the Tam Nong motel (at some

point the music from the video bars did stop; at 3:00 a.m. I crawled out of the mosquito netting and figured out how to turn off the refrigeration unit), we were ready for the birds.

During our three hours in the launch, guided by an earnest young man named Thieng, we saw black drongos, purple herons, grey herons, great egrets, black-shouldered kites, kingfishers, lapwings, swallows, cormorants, and a purple swamp hen. Thieng carried a dog-eared copy of *Birds of Thailand* for reference. He had been on the job for six months; we were his first tourists. Thirty guards, he told us, are hired during crane season to keep local villagers from poaching. We paid fifteen dollars, plus tip, for our excursion.

Thanh—serious Thanh, who seldom smiled—turned out to be our best birder. "Before the war I saw many birds, even near Saigon. But today! I didn't know we had such a place in Vietnam," he exulted.

The crane is symbolic to the Vietnamese of long life, wealth, and happiness, as it is in most Asian cultures. A leggy crane standing on the broad back of a turtle is a revered and popular motif in pagodas and temples. The real-life population of cranes in Dong Thap province had nearly been destroyed during the war. Intent on denying the Viet Cong forest cover, the U.S. military command cut huge drainage channels through the Plain of Reeds. As the wetlands dried out, fires ignited by napalm and other incendiary devices denuded the landscape. Helicopters swooped down on the big birds for fun, bored GIs emptied their rifles at them in "mad minutes," hungry villagers killed them for food. The dried marshland in the area of Tram Chim was spared chemical defoliation, but the parched earth turned abnormally acid.

After the cessation of hostilities, the surviving birds were up against fresh peacetime dangers. A human population explosion—Northerners coming south to look for work, Cambodian refugees crossing the border—impacted on the environment in the form of new settlements, fishing, and farming. Under the government's reforestation program, melaleuca trees (freshwater mangroves) were planted in the former marshlands for their medicinal oils and for timber to build new homes.

The governor of Dong Thap province was a respected former Viet Cong commander known as Muoi Nhe, a *nom de guerre* that translates as "tenth child and scrawny." (He was huge, over six feet two, and had lost an eye in combat.) Remembering the peace and beauty of the marshlands in his childhood, Muoi Nhe was determined to restore a portion to its former state. Vietnam's leading environmentalist, Professor Vo Quy of Hanoi University, an ornithologist by profession, got interested in the idealistic plan. It wasn't feasible to plug the American-made drainage ditches that slashed across the Plain of Reeds, because in the intervening years they had become important waterways for the people in the recovering delta, vital to the transportation of fertilizer, rice, and other produce. But Muoi Nhe and the local farmers constructed a network of dikes around Tram Chim to hold back the floodwaters when the ditches overflowed during the heavy inundations of the rainy season.

Although their budgets are small and their work is quiet, a handful of privately funded groups in the United States and abroad have managed to play a positive role in Vietnam's reconstruction. These nongovernmental organizations, numbering in the hundreds, have served as the only channel for American humanitarian assistance during the past two decades while the trade embargo was being enforced. In 1988 George Archibald of the highly regarded International Crane Foundation in Baraboo, Wisconsin, came to Dong Thap province with German ornithologists from the Brehm Fund for Bird Conservation. Their mission was decidedly unlike that of most other NGOs, which set up prosthesis clinics, nutrition projects, and health programs. The bird people had heard that the sarus crane, an endangered species in Southeast Asia, was returning to the Plain of Reeds.

As it happened, so were the painted stork, the greater adjutant, the Bengal florican, and the black-faced spoonbill, which made a reappearance after the crane habitat began to recover. When the team of international scientists completed their studies, they determined that more elaborate measures were needed to encourage the returning wildlife. A delicate period of negotiations ensued. The Vietnamese were worried that the foreign scientists' strictly environmental concerns would interfere with the country's pragmatic needs.

"Ecosystem management and habitat fragmentation were new concepts for them," says Jeb Barzen, the crane foundation's liaison to Tram Chim. "How and why should they believe our science?" Muoi Nhe was invited to Baraboo to share the American experience in wetland management firsthand.

Eventually the two sides reached a consensus. "This feels like the end of the second Paris peace conference," one of the Vietnamese scientists joked. In a different kind of joint venture than the ones usually bruited about in the *Vietnam Investment Review*, the MacArthur Foundation ponied up money for sluice gates to control the water level at Tram Chim and offered additional funds for a small supervisory staff. The Vietnamese constructed a sturdy field house and exhibition hall. Tram Chim is slated to be declared a national park, the twelfth in the nation. Ecotourism (what I was doing) is to be encouraged.

Birds are no respectors of international boundaries. Ironically, in view of Vietnam's delicate, often uneasy relations with Cambodia, the cranes reside on Khmer turf during their breeding season, when they cleave together in solitary pairs and eat insects and small fish. Ultimately, efforts to protect cranes in Vietnam will have to focus across the border as well.

Maggie and I were received like old friends when we got back to the Continental. Our rooms were ready, our laundry was done. She went out to photograph an evening fashion show at the old opera house. I decided to stay in, watch a video, and nibble Swiss chocolates. At 10:00 p.m. there was a knock on the door. Late-night knocks are always disconcerting. It was a waiter bearing a tray with a piece of tropical fruit, compliments of the management. Green on the outside with sweet white pulp, the delicacy resembled a mangosteen. Its name in Vietnamese translates into "breast milk."

In the breakfast garden the next morning, the crisply dressed woman dining alone (she ordered the breast-milk fruit, I notice) welcomes my company. She is, she says in perfect English, a Viet Kieu—a *returned* Vietnamese—and an executive with Credit Lyonnais, the international French banking house.

"Yes," she laughs, tapping her Montblanc pen, "I was one of those young Saigon girls in miniskirts on the back of a motorbike during the war. Our family left in 1975. We certainly were not Boat People. I didn't become a serious person until I studied finance in Chicago. You're not writing this down, are you?"

I confess that I am, a terrible habit, and ask for her impressions of her native city.

"I would say that Saigon is nearly ninety percent back to what it was before '75. Of course, they try to buy you back emotionally," she frowns, "but the reality is, these people need me."

I suggest that the Canadian businessmen sipping coffee across from us might also benefit from her expertise. This morning the Canadians are looking doleful. Their deal has slid sideways.

"Yes, everything here takes double or triple the time," Ms. Dao Huynh says quietly. "People are cautious, keenly aware of their missed opportunities. But there's a certain inevitability to history, isn't there?"

I answer that I suppose there is, and mention, because they are still on my mind, the young prostitutes at the restaurant in Dong Ha and the glassy-eyed women in their cubicles at the back of the hotel in Cao Lanh.

"Ah yes," she says, perturbed at the direction our conversation has taken. "The pressures from Thailand. This country doesn't yet understand that it is facing an AIDS problem."

And what of the Dickensian beggar children who followed us at China Beach and in the Citadel at Hue, who surrounded our car on the Vinh Long ferry, tapping incessantly, frantically, on the rolled-up window. Vietnam, I'd failed to consider before my trip, had been, and was still, a Third World country with pockets of wealth and an overall poverty that is painful to confront. I am pleased to see people like the Canadians and Ms. Huynh bringing business to a stricken nation that needs it badly, but trickle-down economics is no solution to the growing disparity between rich and poor.

Not that I have any answers. What does a traveler bring to a place, or take from it, except observations?

This is our last morning, and there is so much left to see and do. Tuyen has promised me a ride on his motor scooter if I get back to the hotel before 11:00, when we must leave for the airport. Maggie needs him for more shots of Cholon, so we arrange that I'll go with Thanh and the car to An Quang Pagoda, the last known address of the Venerable Tri Quang, who dropped out of history when General Ky silenced the Buddhists in 1966. But first I want to stop off at Reunification Palace, preserved as it was in 1975 before the abrupt departure of President Thieu.

It's instructive to see how the Thieus lived in stately splendor propped up by American aid: topiary gardens, gaming rooms, trophy rooms, carpeted reception halls with sleek lacquer tables, fine porcelains, sterling silver, crystal chandeliers. A command post in the finished basement. On the top floor of the residence there's a television monitor showing a French-made documentary about the war. I take a seat in the viewing room, fretting about the time. "How far into it are we?" I ask the European couple down the row. The minute it's over I dash downstairs, looking for Thanh.

"Don't worry," calls an amused and cultured European voice. "The last helicopter won't leave without you."

I wince at the clever line.

Thanh drops me off at An Quang Pagoda, a modest stone edifice, crumbling and shabby, on a busy street. I rub my eyes in the sun, overwhelmed to see the simple letters chiseled over the front portal. As easy as that. Seek and you shall find. Ask and you shall receive.

Dear, grave Thanh has loosened up since yesterday's trip to

the nature reserve, when he got so excited about the birds. Frowning and struggling to communicate in English, he tries to tell me a story. "When I worked for You-said," he enunciates with great effort, in stops and starts. "During Diem. They tried to kill Tri Quang. Diem tried to kill him. He escaped over the wall. You-said hid him. In the garage where I worked."

"I remember," I say. "I think I remember."

"I am sorry I cannot go inside with you. I must stay with the car."

"That's okay. It's just a little personal pilgrimage. I'd just as soon go alone."

I run up the few steps and charge inside. What am I doing, out of breath and frantic, in this quiet Buddhist place of worship? What do I hope to find? A woman lighting a joss stick at an altar gives me a quizzical look. A young novice materializes out of nowhere and points to my sandals. I kick them off, stricken with the guilt of a nonbeliever who keeps forgetting the rules. The novice nods politely, tells me he speaks little English, and begins to point out the altars, the statuary, the offerings of food.

Shaking my head, I hurriedly write "Thich Tri Quang" on a piece of paper.

"Tri Quang," he nods. To my confusion, he takes me upstairs. We walk down a long corridor to a wire-mesh enclosure, where he calls out something in Vietnamese.

"He says he'll see you. Come this way." We turn down another corridor, and suddenly I am in a chamber, a monk's simple cell, and there is Tri Quang, sitting cross-legged on the floor. Smiling. A little heavier. Bright, welcoming eyes.

I have not prepared for this moment.

"You are remembered by many people in America," I stutter. "You are a hero."

Smiling beatifically, he says something in Vietnamese. The novice translates. "He says he does not understand."

"Tell him he understands everything." I sense that the audience is over, that I should back out the door.

"Come back tomorrow," the novice calls after me when I've retrieved my shoes.

ACKNOWLEDGMENTS

A score of people opened my eyes to Vietnam before I set foot in the country. Here are some of their names: Kevin Cooney, Merle Ratner, Sys Morch, and Nora Taylor. My gratitude goes to Barbara Peck and Ila Stanger of *Travel & Leisure* for giving me the original magazine assignment. Hilda Gore entrusted me with her husband Leo Cawley's Vietnam library. Leo was a marine at Khe Sanh who died in July 1991 of multiple myeloma he believed was Agent Orange–related.

Sarah Timewell of InnerAsia and Kat Callo of Reuters gave me a big assist in Hanoi. Huu Thinh, Nguyen Quang Thieu, and Le Minh Khue of Hanoi's *Van Nghe* weekly added to my understanding on their trip to New York.

Of the many good people I met at the fourth annual U.S. NGO Forum on Viet Nam, Cambodia and Laos, June 17–20, 1993, I especially want to thank Ed Murphy, Dan Duffy, Kevin Bowen, John McAuliff, Dr. Arnold Schecter, Nguyen Ngoc Hung, Thon Thi Ngoc Du, and Sandra Wittman.

Lillian Lent of the Frances Goldin Agency, and Frances Goldin herself, read and critiqued chapters as I wrote them. Jim Spencer gave the entire manuscript a close reading and corrected some boners. *Cam on*, Jim.

Some of my sources are not apparent in the text. Key works include: William S. Turley and Mark Selden, eds., *Reinventing Vietnamese Socialism: Doi Moi in Comparative Perspective*, Westview Press, 1993; Neil L. Jamieson, Nguyen

Manh Hung, and A. Terry Rambo, eds., *The Challenges of Vietnam's Reconstruction*, a joint publication of the Indochina Institute, George Mason University, Fairfax, Virginia, and the East-West Center Indochina Initiative, Honolulu, Hawaii, 1992; Mya Than and Joseph L. H. Tan, *Vietnam's Dilemmas and Options*, Institute of Southeast Asian Studies, Singapore, 1993; Elizabeth Kempf, *Month of Pure Light: The Regreening of Vietnam*, The Women's Press, 1990; Marilyn Young, *The Vietnam Wars*, HarperCollins, 1991; Ngo Vinh Long, *Before the Revolution: The Vietnamese Peasants under the French*, Columbia University Press, 1991; John Prados and Ray W. Stubbe, *Valley of Decision: The Siege of Khe Sanh*, Dell, 1991; Doan Van Toai and David Chanoff, *The Vietnamese Gulag*, Simon & Schuster, 1986; John DeFrancis, *Colonialism and Language Policy in Viet Nam*, Mouton Publishers, The Hague, 1977; Jean Lacouture, *Ho Chi Minh*, Vintage Books, 1968; John Guy, *Ceramic Traditions of South-East Asia*, Oxford University Press, 1989; Nicole Routhier, *The Foods of Vietnam*, Stewart, Tabori & Chang, 1989.

Joyce Johnson, Ken Siman, and Peggy Hadden augmented my reading material. Merle Geline Rubine came up with good sources. Barbara Probst Solomon suggested the title.

At HarperCollins I was lucky to be in the firm editorial grip of Joy Johannessen, the well-known archangel.